# REPORTERS ON THE BATTLEFIELD

## The Embedded Press System in Historical Context

Christopher Paul • James J. Kim

NATIONAL SECURITY RESEARCH DIVISION

This report results from the RAND Corporation's continuing program of self-initiated research. Support for such research is provided, in part, by donors and by the independent research and development provisions of RAND's contracts for the operation of its U.S. Department of Defense federally funded research and development centers.

**Library of Congress Cataloging-in-Publication Data**

Paul, Christopher, 1971–
Reporters on the battlefield : the embedded press system in historical context / Christopher Paul, James J. Kim.
p. cm.
Includes bibliographical references.
"MG-200."
ISBN 0-8330-3654-8 (pbk.)
1. War—Press coverage. 2. Iraq War, 2003—Press coverage. I. Kim, James J. II. Title.

PN4784.W37P38 2004
070.4'333—dc22

2004019522

The RAND Corporation is a nonprofit research organization providing objective analysis and effective solutions that address the challenges facing the public and private sectors around the world. RAND's publications do not necessarily reflect the opinions of its research clients and sponsors.



*Cover design by Stephen Bloodsworth*



Published 2004 by the RAND Corporation
1776 Main Street, P.O. Box 2138, Santa Monica, CA 90407-2138
1200 South Hayes Street, Arlington, VA 22202-5050
201 North Craig Street, Suite 202, Pittsburgh, PA 15213-1516
RAND URL: http://www.rand.org/
To order RAND documents or to obtain additional information, contact
Distribution Services: Telephone: (310) 451-7002;
Fax: (310) 451-6915; Email: order@rand.org

# Preface

While the history of relations between the press and the military predates modern journalism, much of what had gone before was neutralized by the horrible press-military breakdown that occurred during U.S. involvement in Vietnam. By the end of the Vietnam War, press-military trust was at an all time low, and antagonism on both sides at an all time high. Many in the press, feeling repeatedly misled, reported ongoing events in an unfavorable light; many in the military felt betrayed by this "inappropriate" and negative press coverage and wanted to have nothing further to do with the press. Following Vietnam, the tension between First Amendment protections, generally accepted citizen "right to know," and military resistance and desire for operational secrecy has led press-military relations through several different institutional forms. First, the complete exclusion of the press from the intervention in Grenada, followed by the better but less-than-satisfactory "press pool" systems used in Panama and during the first Gulf War, and the "turning of the tables" in Haiti and Somalia, where the press was in country before the troops, concluding (for the present) with the "embedded press" system, in which journalists are attached to, and travel with specific military units. The embedded press system appears to be the best solution to date at balancing the needs of the three core constituencies (the press, the military, and the public); the questions remain whether that appearance is correct, what improvements remain to be made, and what, if any, vulnerabilities (for any of the constituents) the embedded press system creates.

This research focuses on the embedded press system deployed during Operation Iraqi Freedom and should be of interest to those in the armed forces, the media, policymakers responsible for regulating press access, as well as the public at large. It attempts to answer the following questions: How effective was the embedded press system in meeting the needs of the three main constituencies (the press, the military, and the citizens of the United States)? What policy history led to the innovation of an embedded press system? Where are press-military relations likely to go in the future? These questions are answered through an evaluation of the embedded press system, a set of lessons learned from press-military relations during the recent conflict, and an analysis of the strengths and weaknesses of the embedded press system (or its descendants) for possible future operations.

This research was conducted within the International Security and Defense Policy Center (ISDP) of the National Security Research Division (NSRD), a unit of the RAND Corporation. NSRD conducts research and analysis for the Office of the Secretary of Defense, the Joint Staff, the Unified Commands, the defense agencies, the Department of the Navy, the U.S. intelligence community, allied foreign governments, and foundations.

This book results from the RAND Corporation's continuing program of self-initiated research. Support for such research is provided, in part, by donors and by the independent research and development provisions of RAND's contracts for the operation of its U.S. Department of Defense federally funded research and development centers.

For more information on the RAND International Security and Defense Policy Center, contact the director, James Dobbins. He can be reached at James_Dobbins@rand.org; 310-393-0411, ext. 5134; RAND Corporation, 1700 Main Street, Santa Monica, California 90407-2138.

# Contents

# Figures

# Tables

# Summary

The March 2003 U.S. invasion of Iraq coincided with the first broad implementation of an innovative means of wartime coverage known as "embedded press." Under this system, over 600 reporters from a diverse range of American and international news organizations were "embedded" in U.S. military units, i.e., they traveled with the soldiers in their units, saw what the soldiers saw, and were under fire when troops were—all while bringing live televised coverage of the war into living rooms around the world.

Although the embedded press system has been heralded as a great success, no systematic evaluation of this system has yet been undertaken. This research seeks to address this need by examining the role of the embedded press in Iraq within the broader context of historical press-military relations. In particular, we focus on the tensions arising from long-standing differences between the military and the press with regard to the dissemination of information during wartime: While the military is focused chiefly on preventing information of value from falling into enemy hands, the press aims to broadcast the full story to the public.

To examine the role of the embedded press, we have constructed an evaluative framework that considers the goals of the press, the military, and the public—the three relevant constituencies for press-military relations. We use this framework to develop a set of measures for evaluating the embedded press system in relation to other options for organizing press-military relations as revealed through comparative case studies. We have conducted preliminary analyses, where possible, using these methods, which will be appropriate for future systematic analyses.

## The Potential for Conflict Arises from the Different Missions of the Press and the Military

As is to be expected, the press and the military have different missions and characteristics, as well as different goals with regard to wartime news coverage. These differences are highlighted in Table S.1. Of special significance is the contrast between the press's focus on its mission of reporting and the military's focus on its operational mission. The press's interest in gaining access to information so that it can inform the public (both to fulfill its obligations to the public and to garner profits and/or ratings for its parent organization) can come into direct conflict with the military's need to ensure operational and informational security.

Despite these key differences, the military and the press do share certain commonalities. Both aspire to a high level of professionalism, and both focus on serving the public, albeit in very different ways. The military exists to defend and protect the United States and its territories, while the press exists to keep the public informed; both roles are considered critical to a healthy democracy. But while both institutions serve the public interest, there is a tension between reporters' need for access to information and the military's need to maintain operational security. Surveys have shown that, in resolving this tension, the public has consistently favored the military's need for operational security over the press' desire for full disclosure. Nonetheless, the public also has goals of receiving a high level of war coverage and in being "well-served" by such coverage.

**Table S.1**
**Comparison of Press and Military Missions and Goals**

| Press | Military |
|---|---|
| | **Mission** |
| Reporting | Protection and defense of the United States |
| | **Mission-Related Goals** |
| Uphold obligations to the public<br>Achieve profits | Achieve operational success<br>Maintain operational security |
| | **Organizational Attributes** |
| Horizontal/competitive<br>Reflexive<br>Reactive<br>Professional | Hierarchical/cooperative<br>Reflexive<br>Reactive and Proactive<br>Professional |
| | **Goals for News Coverage** |
| Gain access to newsworthy information<br>Provide newsworthy information to the public<br>Fulfill obligations to the public<br>Build market share<br>Maintain quality of news<br>Objectivity (tell both sides of the story)<br>Accuracy<br>Credibility | Do not allow news coverage to compromise operational security<br>Fulfill legal obligations regarding press access<br>Use news coverage to support military mission<br>Obtain good public relations<br>Build credibility<br>Support information operations |

## Tensions Between the Press and the Military Have Led to a Variety of Press Access Strategies

The history of press-military relations illustrates several critical junctures in the trajectory of their interactions. In Vietnam, the press enjoyed high levels of access to operations, largely because of the relatively amicable relationship that had developed between the press and the military, particularly in World War II. However, this relationship experienced a significant shift during the Vietnam War, as news coverage critical of both the war and the military engendered tensions. The legacy of these tensions significantly influenced press-military relations in later operations in Grenada and Panama. Another notable shift occurred during the first Gulf War, however, establishing the basis for new kinds of press access, which ultimately led to the embedded press system used during major combat operations in Iraq in 2003.

## Embedded Press Is One of Several Options for Organizing Press-Military Relations

The embedded press system can be considered along a continuum of idealized options for organizing press-military relations, each of which involves a particular strategy for press access. At one end of the continuum for press access is *denial of access*, under which press coverage is limited to official sources only. *Press pools* represent a somewhat more open system of access, under which a small number of preselected reporters are allowed access to some otherwise unavailable sources of information; in exchange for that access, reporters pool their resources with each other. As already noted, *embedded press* means that reporters travel with military units, seeing what they see. At the other end of the continuum is *unilateral journalism*. Under this strategy, reporters operate with broad freedom of access, either by freely joining or leaving troops in the field and traveling on any military vehicle with space available; or by participating in the more freeform "cowboy" or "four-wheel-drive" journalism, in which reporters reject both the constraint of traveling with the military and any military-imposed constraints on access.

Access strategies typically interact with different operational security strategies, including credentialing, under which reporters agree on their professional honor not to violate the confidence of the military; censorship, in which the military unilaterally decides that certain information cannot be released to the public; and "security at the source," under which military personnel agree to be circumspect in deciding what information to share with reporters.

To evaluate the success of the embedded press, we developed a series of measures based on the military and press goals highlighted above, as well as additional measures related to the public's interests. A full list of outcomes and measures can be found in Table 4.3 on pp. 73–74. In comparing systems for press-military relations, we considered the ways in which access strategies can interact with different operational security strategies.

## The Embedded Press System Can be Judged as Widely Successful Across a Broad Range of Outcomes and Measures

### Military Outcomes

*Do not allow news coverage to compromise operational security.* Although, in the abstract, embedded press is one of the most vulnerable systems of press-military relations from an operational security standpoint, our research found that, given the potential magnitude of the threat, operational security during the major combat operations phase of Operation Iraqi Freedom (OIF) was generally intact and protected far more than it was violated. At the same time, operational security was not perfect, nor was it close to the military's target threshold of "secure." Available evidence indicates that there were fewer than half a dozen "disembeddings" for violations of operational security, and there was no evidence of any compromises of operational security in which Iraqi forces took advantage of violations of security.

*Fulfill legal obligations regarding press access.* Embedded press as implemented in Iraq succeeded well in terms of fulfilling legal obligations. Perhaps at risk to operational security, the military gave broad access to troops and fighting, while the embedded press made great quantities of information available to the public, who followed the war closely.

*Obtain good public relations.* The embedded press in Iraq, coupled with the decisive military victory and the by-and-large exemplary performance of U.S. forces, resulted in excellent public relations for the military. Perhaps the only exception was negative coverage during the second week of the war. News coverage of the major combat operations phase was carried out with far fewer press complaints than seen in previous major conventional operations, such as those in Grenada, Panama, and the first Gulf War.

*Build credibility.* The analysis suggested that the military was very careful to protect its credibility, and it was reasonably successful at doing so. Although vague or tentative information released in U.S. Central Command briefings may have irked the press, the military took care to avoid making erroneous claims and carefully qualified the language of uncertainty when relaying unverified reports.

*Support information operations.* Operation Iraqi Freedom contained two main examples of the military's successful incorporation of press coverage in "honest" information operations. The "shock and awe" campaign at the beginning of the war made the press a willing participant in showing the advancing might of U.S. armed forces; while this display did not result in complete Iraqi submission, it likely had some effect, although this is difficult to measure. Press coverage was also used effectively to debunk false claims made by the Iraqi Minister of Information.

**Press Outcomes**

*Establish a satisfactory access arrangement.* The embedded press system as implemented allowed the press unprecedented access. The system used in Iraq included not only the embedded press, but other forms of press access, including unilateral reporting and official information releases from the U.S. Central Command.

*Ensure reporter safety.* In general, risks to reporters under an embedded press system were comparable to the risks to the soldiers they were accompanying. The number of reporters killed during the main combat phase of Operation Iraqi Freedom was thirteen, four of whom were embedded reporters. Given the relative number of embedded versus unilateral reporters, embedding in Iraq was safer than reporting unilaterally, but still risky.

*Fulfill obligations to the public.* The public generally approved of the coverage of the major combat operations phase of OIF. While public approval almost certainly results from a variety of factors beyond the issue of whether or not the public receives sufficient information to exercise their democratic rights, approval can reasonably be imputed at least in part from the information's effectiveness in helping people exercise those rights.

*Build market share.* While we did not seek data about the relative market success of different press agencies, poll data asking respondents about their sources of information on the war suggest that the embedded press system created conditions favorable to live television coverage. It is unclear whether this type of coverage was viewed at the expense of, or in addition to, other news formats.

*Maintain quality journalism.* Our view—based on public opinion data, a study by the Project for Excellence in Journalism, and news analysis—suggests that coverage of major combat operations during OIF was generally of "good" quality, although there was room for improvement. In particular, our historical narrative revealed several concerns with journalistic quality during major combat operations in Iraq—most related to fears of patriotic bias or to the potential for embedded reporters to lose their objectivity because of their companionship with troops.

*Build credibility.* Public opinion polls suggest that coverage of major combat operations during OIF improved the perception of the media among some members of the public, but worsened the perception among others. Many felt that reporters were too eager to paint either a negative or a positive picture of the war, suggesting a baseline expectation of bias that is not consonant with high credibility.

### Public Outcomes

*Public satisfaction, information, and service.* Several public opinion polls suggest that, by and large, the public was well satisfied with wartime coverage.

## The Embedded Press System Is Not Without Future Risks

A comparison of the embedded press with other systems of press-military relations used in previous conflicts suggests that, although, in general, a combination of embedded press and unilateral journalism has favorable or positive outcomes across the board, there are still potential risks involved, particularly to operational security and reporter safety. Such risks can be mitigated to a large extent through a system of credentials to register and to screen reporters, such as that used in Iraq.

The use of the embedded press system in future operations could raise additional risks as follows, which also need to be mitigated:

- *Legacies of previous conflicts.* What has gone before matters. Given the successes of the embedded press system in the war in Iraq, the majority of stakeholders from the military, press, and public will expect to see some form of this system used in the next major U.S. military operation; should that fail to occur, certain expected "relationship" outcomes, such as military public relations with the press and the public, are likely to be diminished simply because of disappointed expectations.
- *Developments in technology.* Given the changes wrought by technological innovations such as the real-time global coverage made possible by advances in portable satellite-based communications, it is not inconceivable that some future innovation will further change the nature of coverage and force innovation and change in future press-military relations.
- *Planning and lead time.* Longer lead times afford planners the opportunity to consider press relations well in advance and develop appropriate access strategies. Anything that shortens the time the press has to prepare (such as crisis operations or secrecy) creates constraints on the implementation of certain press systems, including the potential for embedding reporters.
- *Nature of operations.* The nature of a military operation can have an important impact on several press-military outcomes. For example, air wars and special operations can be difficult for the press to cover effectively. Also, as the quality of opposing forces increases, so too do the risks to operational security and the danger to reporters posed by embedding.

- *The value of victory.* Systems of press-military relations such as the embedded press system rely heavily on the ability of U.S. forces to successfully complete their missions with a minimum of errors. Victory all but assures the military of good public relations with the population at large and increases the likelihood of good relations with the press if it is coupled with broad press access. In contrast, when military operations go poorly, press-military relations can come under severe strain, especially if the press has been granted broad access.

## Recommendations for Addressing Other Possible Shortcomings of the Embedded Press System

Our analysis led us to identify several recommendations for addressing potential problems with the use of embedded press in future operations.

- The embedded press system creates a hierarchy of credentials between embedded reporters and unilateral reporters. To avoid potential resentments and related problems, future systems would do well to consider credentialing and validating unilateral reporters to some extent.
- Although embedded reporters get a close-up view of operations, that view is also somewhat narrow, producing what has been called a "soda-straw effect." This effect can be mitigated to the extent that the public has access to the views provided by many "soda straws." Also, editors or producers can help to ensure that these views are synthesized into easily digestible reports. In addition, embedding should continue to be supplemented by other systems of press access that provide different perspectives.
- Some believe that the embedded press system can lead reporters to lose their objectivity because they identify too closely with the soldiers with whom they are embedded. Given the myriad pressures and possible sources of bias that are brought to bear on reporters every day, we did not find the potential bias inherent in

the embedding process to be of great concern; however, further research may be warranted.

- The effects of technology and the 24-hour news cycle should not be underestimated. Coverage provided by the embedded press, together with increases in other forms of media coverage, can exaggerate both good and bad news. Increased coverage makes information available to the public that had previously been available only to military personnel, in some cases resulting in pressure on political and military authorities to respond more quickly than in the past. This is a real concern for decisionmakers and field commanders alike and may not serve the public interest.
- With the embedded press system, the extent to which risks to operational security are mitigated depends to a large extent on the integrity and professionalism of reporters. In order to ensure that reporters can fulfill their obligations, it will be important for news organizations to assign experienced journalists to combat operations and to make these reporters familiar with military operations in advance of their embedding.

# Acknowledgments

We would like to thank our RAND colleagues Nelson Lim, Susan Everingham, Rachel Swanger, and Jeffrey Isaacson for their support and encouragement in undertaking this research. For their helpful feedback and suggestions, we thank the participants in a RAND seminar presenting preliminary findings for this book. Special thanks to the several reporters and military officers who shared their thoughts and experiences with us; we would thank them each by name but wish to protect their anonymity.

We also wish to extend our thanks to Eric Larson for allowing us to use his data on public opinion and media coverage. Thanks, too, to Jack Snyder, Anibal Perez-Liñan, and Brigitte Nacos for their helpful comments and feedback on drafts of early parts of this work. Thanks to Eric Larson and *Pittsburgh Tribune-Review* reporter Carl Prine for their helpful reviews of this document during the quality assurance process.

We truly appreciate the help and support of administrative assistant Maria Falvo, RAND librarian Judy Lesso, and research communicator Kristin Leuschner; each of them made an invaluable contribution to our ability to produce this book in this form. Any errors that remain are the authors' alone.

CHAPTER ONE

# Introduction

> The first essential in military operations is that no information of value shall be given to the enemy. The first essential in newspaper work and broadcasting is wide-open publicity. It is your job and mine to try to reconcile those sometimes diverse considerations.
>
> — Dwight D. Eisenhower[1]

## The Origins of "Embedded Press"

The March 2003 U.S. invasion of Iraq coincided with the first broad implementation of an innovative means of wartime coverage: "embedded press." Over 600 reporters from a diverse range of American and international news organizations were "embedded" in U.S. military units, i.e., they traveled with the troops in their units, ate with them, and were billeted with them; they saw what the soldiers saw, were under fire when the troops were, and endured the same hardships (combat, heat, sand storms, long days on the move). Perhaps most remarkable and consequential, they brought live coverage of all of these things through the television into the living rooms of most homes throughout the world.

[1] Dwight D. Eisenhower, 1944, quoted in *Conduct of the Persian Gulf War*, Washington, D.C.: Office of the Secretary of Defense, Final Report to Congress, April 1992, p. 651. Online at http://www.ndu.edu/library/epubs/cpgw.pdf (as of September 23, 2003).

In the aftermath of major combat operations[2], the embedded press system has been heralded as a great success.[3] Pentagon spokeswoman Victoria Clarke, in describing the embedded press system, has asserted that "this will be the model now, I believe, unless you know otherwise, for the future."[4] Time will tell if this proves to be the case.

Despite the apparent success of the embedded press model, long-standing differences exist between the military and the press, as indicated by the quotation that begins this chapter. A key issue concerns the different priorities of the military and the press, the former working to prevent "information of value" from falling into enemy hands, the latter seeking to make the "full story" known to the public.

This book seeks to examine the role of the embedded press system within the context of the historical tensions surrounding military-press relations. We focus on two key issues:

- Given the history of tension in press-military relations and the range of previous wartime press policies, how did embedded press come about?
- Do the properties of the embedded press system warrant its popularity? In other words, how well did the embedded press succeed in meeting the goals of the military and the press for wartime reporting? And how does embedded press compare with other systems for organizing military-press relations?

---

[2] On May 1, 2003, President George W. Bush declared an end to major combat operations in Iraq. While Operation Iraqi Freedom (OIF) is ongoing as a low-intensity conflict and reconstruction effort as of this writing, the system of formal embedding that constituted "embedded press" ended shortly after major combat operations in Iraq concluded and embedded reporters left their embedding units to return to traditional reporting techniques. Throughout this book, references to press coverage during "the recent war in Iraq," or "Operation Iraqi Freedom (OIF)" refer only to the less than six weeks of major combat operations.

[3] Brookings Institution, *Assessing Media Coverage of the War in Iraq: Press Reports, Pentagon Rules, and Lessons for the Future,* A Brookings Iraq Series Briefing, Falk Auditorium, Washington, D.C., June 17, 2003.

[4] Quoted in Brookings, *Assessing Media Coverage of the War in Iraq.*

With those questions in mind, this research attempts to meet several interrelated goals. Through a thoughtful consideration of the history of press-military relations, we construct an evaluative framework that considers the goals of three relevant constituencies: the press, the military, and the public. We use this framework to evaluate the embedded press system in relation to other options for organizing press-military relations, both in general and in specific historical contexts. We hope that our approach can be used as the basis for more systematic future analyses of press-military relations, and to that end, we identify tools, methods, and measures appropriate for future research.

## Defining the Key Constituencies in Military-Press Relations

Having laid out the broad goals of our research, we now define the core constituencies that are central to this effort: the press, the military, and the public.

As it is used here, "press" denotes a wide range of different types of media and media organizations. Although the term "press" has its origins in print culture, we are using the term to refer to anyone involved in the production of news in various media: producers, editors, anchors, reporters, crews, etc. "Press" will be used to denote all of these individuals collectively and separately in their roles as journalists, but the term is also intended to recognize the atomized and competing nature of news agencies and reporters: As discussed in Chapter Two, the press is composed of individuals who can interpret their jobs, goals, roles, and obligations in very different ways. We do restrict our discussion to the mainstream press but, in doing so, do not mean to imply homogeneity among those in the mainstream press.

While we emphasize the heterogeneity of the press, our definition of "military" acknowledges that the hierarchical and cooperative nature of the services (see Chapter Two) lends validity to a uniform and unified treatment. Nonetheless, although the military can be viewed as monolithic, we recognize that the existence of a uniform military policy does not mean that everyone in the military agrees with the policy or will implement it in the same way. As will be discussed in Chapters Three, Four, and Five, the views and actions of individuals in the military at both the highest levels and lower levels of command can have important effects on the implementation or outcomes of policies governing press-military relations. "Military" in this research is used inclusively to denote both uniformed and civilian personnel, including those in the Pentagon, officers and enlisted soldiers from all services, the Secretary of Defense, and all elements of the Office of the Secretary of Defense and the Department of Defense (DoD).

Finally, "public" is used here inclusively but also (intentionally) somewhat vaguely. While our focus is clearly on the U.S. domestic public (we use "international public" when necessary for clarity), we are generally leaving "the public" undefined in order to consider a wide range of theoretical claims about different publics without being limited to any particular notion of public that might match some definitional assumption. Further, we believe that different elements of the military and the press define "public" differently, and we want to be able to consider any of these definitions.

## Methods

This book relies primarily on comparative historical case studies. For all cases preceding Operation Iraqi Freedom (OIF), case studies are based on sources from the rich secondary literature in military history and policy history. For the case of OIF, given that the secondary literature has had virtually no time to form, the case has been constructed from primary sources.

The evaluation relies on a careful case study of the embedded press system as used during the major combat operations phase of OIF, including the planning process, as documented in news articles in the archives of major newspapers, official Pentagon press releases, and documented meetings and conferences involving press and Pentagon representatives.

While historical methods can offer compelling explanations and nuanced analyses, proper "evaluation" requires quantitative measurement. This book identifies a set of outcomes for the evaluation of systems of press-military relations and proposes rigorous quantitative measures for those outcomes. In addition to the comparative historical analysis that forms the core of this book, we present findings drawn from existing public opinion surveys and other poll data collected by prominent polling organizations.

## Significance of this Research

This study makes several new scholarly contributions. First and foremost, it analyzes the relationship between the press and the military in a way that no previous works have. We argue for the need to take this interaction seriously, i.e., to identify the *problem(s)* inherent to this relationship and to attempt to solve them. Regardless of how it fits into causal arguments, the relationship between the press and the military is dynamic and poorly understood, and the problems inherent in this relationship can be best examined through a thoughtful analytic approach. Second, using a systematic analytic framework, this book presents an evaluation of the embedded press system, a notionally new and newly implemented system, and presents some preliminary findings based on that framework. We believe that this work breaks new ground in this regard.

Third, we present case histories that provide two new and important contributions. Our analysis of the case studies focuses not so much on the extensive details of specific cases as on the "connecting events"—i.e., the activities and interplay between the press and the military that occur after one major deployment and prior to another—the interstices between the "cases." Finally, this book contains methodological suggestions for more rigorous research based on the developed analytic framework and proposed outcomes and measures.

## Structure of the Book

The remainder of the book is structured as follows: Chapter Two presents a discussion of the relationship between the press and the military by considering the mission and characteristics of each as well as their respective goals with regard to wartime news coverage. Chapter Three illustrates the development of the embedded press system by presenting a series of case studies drawn from the history of U.S. press-military relations, up to and including Operation Iraqi Freedom. Chapter Four identifies a range of options for organizing press-military relations and presents a series of relevant measures for evaluating and comparing systems of press-military relations. Chapter Five offers a preliminary analysis of the embedded press system relative to other ways in which press-military relations can be organized, in both historical and hypothetical contexts. Chapter Six presents our conclusions regarding the future of press-military relations and the embedded press system. Lastly, two appendixes present more-detailed discussions on the public's "right to know" and the various methods we propose to collect data for evaluating systems of press-military relations.

CHAPTER TWO

# The Relationship Between the Press and the Military: A Starting Point

> At their worst the military wraps itself in the flag and the media wrap themselves in the First Amendment and neither party listens to the other.
>
> — Peter Andrews[1]

Numerous scholars begin their discussion of press-military relations from the premise that the two institutions are inherently different in both their nature and goals.[2] Although some of the more nuanced analyses recognize the contribution of specific historical antecedents to the oft-observed tension between the press and the military, all suggest that these "inherent" differences result in "inevitable" tension and conflict. Steger's description is typical of this point of view:

> The military and the press are two institutions which, to a degree, are inherently opposed to each other. The military values

---

[1] Andrews, Peter, "The Media and the Military," *American Heritage,* Vol. 42, No. 4, July 1991, p. 79.

[2] See, for example, Andrews, "The Media and the Military"; Steger, Michael D., "Slicing the Gordian Knot: A Proposal to Reform Military Regulation of Media Coverage of Combat Operations," *University of San Francisco Law Review,* Vol. 287, Summer 1994, pp. 957–1007; Hickey, Neil, "Access Denied: Pentagon's War Reporting Rules Are Toughest Ever," *Columbia Journalism Review,* Vol. 40, No. 5, Jan./Feb. 2002, pp. 26–31; Porch, Douglas, "No Bad Stories," *Naval War College Review,* Vol. 55, No. 1, Winter 2002, pp. 85–107. Online at http://www.nwc.navy.mil/press/review/2002/winter/art5%2Dw02.htm (as of September 23, 2003).

> an organized chain of command, loyalty, sacrifice and secrecy. The press, on the other hand, stresses individualism, the questioning of authority, skepticism, openness, and a perpetual search for "truth." These two different institutional outlooks create inevitable tensions between the military and the press.[3]

Steger's description seems to ring true, though it certainly is not an exhaustive description of the two institutions. Can a more extensive set of characteristics and differences be enumerated, and are those differences sufficient to make tension "inevitable"?

This chapter addresses these questions by introducing the foundational issues relevant to the relationship between the press and the military. We begin by describing the missions of the two institutions as well as the respective mission-related goals and institutional characteristics of each. We then focus on the goals of each institution for wartime news coverage. A discussion of these goals allows us to make several observations on the relationship between the press and the military. The chapter concludes by considering the relationship of the press and the military vis-à-vis the third core constituency, the public.

## The Press

### Mission Focus: Reporting

Obviously, the main mission of the press is to collect, edit, and report the news.[4] This role has its foundation in the First Amendment right

---

[3] Steger, "Slicing the Gordian Knot," p. 957.

[4] While we offer a working definition of the press in Chapter One, we wish to briefly highlight the contribution of the singular work of Michael Schudson on the nature of news and of the press (Schudson, Michael, *The Power of News*, Cambridge, Mass.: Harvard University Press, 1995). Schudson's discussion of the press contains several key points that have contributed to our understanding of military-press relations, the most important of which is the historically and socially determined nature of reporting and news. He asserts that the social construction of news has resulted in several significant traditions of modern journalism, including how news is categorized (local, national, foreign; general news, business, sports, and features), what is considered interesting or unusual, how to evidence or validate a claim, what constitutes a legitimate source, and how to construct a news story. Several other key observations from Schudson's work appear in our discussion in this section.

to a free press. In its reporting role, the press serves as a form of "witness" to the acts of the government.

> So long as information is publicly available, political actors have to behave *as if* someone in the public is paying attention. Contemporary American journalism presumes that the public is eavesdropping; even if the public is absent, the assumption of public presence makes all the difference [emphasis in original].[5]

The press's reporting mission leads to two broad goals that guide its activities. First is the role the press serves as the "4th Estate." This term has its origin in the growing importance of reporters in late 19th and early 20th century Britain, a role that led Thomas Carlyle to claim that reporters constituted a fourth branch of Parliament.[6] The notion of the press as the 4th Estate has continued relevance in the context of the contemporary United States, in that the press, although not a formal part of the government, continues to play an important role for democracy by reporting on the process and outcomes of the government.

Another broad goal relating to the press's mission is the profit motive. This goal derives from the fact that, at core, the various entities constituting the press are *businesses* and must, in some fundamental sense, act in a businesslike manner. Ownership and business-

---

[5] Schudson, *The Power of News*, p. 25.

[6] As Thomas Carlyle said in 1905, building on statements by Edmund Burke:

> Burke said there were Three Estates in Parliament; but in the Reporters' Gallery yonder, there sat a Fourth Estate more important than they all. It is not a figure of speech or a witty saying; it is a literal fact. . . . Printing, which comes necessarily out of writing, I say often, is equivalent to Democracy. . . . Whoever can speak, speaking now to the whole nation, becomes a power, a branch of government, with inalienable weight in lawmaking, in all acts of authority. It matters not what rank he has, what revenues or garnitures: the requisite thing is that he have a tongue which others will listen to; this and nothing more is requisite.

related concerns have been shown to have an impact on story selection,[7] format decisions,[8] and presentation of news content.[9]

Some scholars take the cynical stance that the profit motive is the *sole* goal of the press, [10] but we reject that formulation as being too simplistic. Others, such as Schudson, have noted that the profit motive can lead to "serious defects in American journalism."[11] Without necessarily accepting the value judgment explicit in the notion of "serious defects," we can accept the profit motive as inherent in the mission of the press, and pursuit of profits as a key goal of the press as a business.

### Institutional Characteristics

Although the press consists of many organizations, these entities—when considered together—tend to share certain institutional attributes or characteristics, which we will describe in this subsection. Drawing from Aukofer and Lawrence, Schudson, and several others, we have chosen to focus on the following characteristics: the press is by nature horizontal/competitive, reflexive, reactive, and professional.

**Horizontal/Competitive.** By "horizontal" we mean to suggest that the press is not part of a single structure or hierarchy. As noted in the introduction, "the press" as used here refers to thousands of reporters working for hundreds of different news outlets, each with potentially different aims and goals, and different views of what it

---

[7] Epstein, Edward Jay, *News from Nowhere*, Chicago: Ivan R. Dee, 1973.

[8] Underwood, Douglas, *When MBAs Rule the Newsroom: How the Marketers and Managers Are Reshaping Today's Media*, New York: Columbia University Press, 1993.

[9] Bennett, W. Lance, *News: The Politics of Illusion (2nd edition)*, White Plains, NY: Longman, 1988. More cynical views have focused on the vulnerability of news agencies to Pentagon leverage as a result of DoD contracts with news agencies' parent companies. For example, MacArthur and Bagdikian contend that, during the first Gulf War, NBC was vulnerable to intimidation by the Pentagon because of all the (potentially vulnerable) defense contracts held by General Electric, which owned NBC (MacArthur, John R., and Ben H. Bagdikian, *Second Front: Censorship and Propaganda in the Gulf War,* Berkeley, Calif.: University of California Press, 1993, pp. 220–221.)

[10] Chomsky, Noam, and Edward Herman, *Manufacturing Consent: The Political Economy of the Mass Media*, New York: Pantheon, 1988, for example.

[11] Schudson, *The Power of News*, p. 4.

means to be part of "the press." Even when core press "goals" can be distilled, different press representatives will likely choose to pursue them in individual ways. Moreover, even within individual news agencies, the management structure tends to be "flatter" than in most businesses or organizations, with many reporters all at roughly the same "level," reporting to comparatively few editors or managers.

Further contributing to this horizontal nature is the competition among and within news agencies. Different media outlets compete for access, stories, and "scoops." Individual reporters compete for journalistic prizes and acknowledgements, as well as for promotions and choice assignments.

Besides the competitiveness inherent in the context of financially competitive news outlets, news coverage by nature tends to focus on conflict. Journalistic convention maintains that there are two sides to every story; news following this convention can create the appearance of conflict even in its absence.[12]

The press willingly embraces an adversarial position as part of its public mission. Reporter James Reston asserts,

> The rising power of the United States in world affairs requires not a more compliant press, but a relentless barrage of facts and criticism. Our job in this age, as I see it, is not to serve as cheerleaders for our side, but to help the largest possible number of people to see the realities.[13]

---

[12] Schudson, *The Power of News*, p. 9.

[13] As quoted in Council on Foreign Relations, *Embedded Journalists in Iraq: Reality TV or Desert Mirage?* Transcript, Co-sponsored with the College of William and Mary, Washington, D.C., July 29, 2003. Online at http://www.cfr.org/publication.php?id=6189# (as of September 23, 2003). This, actually, is not a novel notion; the idea dates back to Benjamin Franklin ("Apology for Printers," in *Benjamin Franklin: Writings,* New York: Library of America, 1987, p. 172) who wrote the following:

> That the Opinions of Men are almost as various as their Faces; an Observation general enough to become a common Proverb, "So many Men so many Minds." . . . Printers are educated in the Belief, that when Men differ in Opinion, both Sides ought equally to have the Advantage of being heard by the Publick; and that when Truth and Error have fair Play, the former is always an overmatch for the latter: Hence they chearfully [sic] serve all contending Writers that pay them well, without regarding on which side they are of the Question in Dispute.

In addition, Schudson notes the particular vigor with which the American press pursues scandals.[14]

**Reflexive.** As a profession, journalism is generally reflexive—i.e., journalists engage in regular dialogue on the nature and quality of news coverage and give considerable attention to violations of journalistic ethics (or perceived violations).[15] These dialogues are very often public and can themselves become journalistic content. Journalists do not always reach consensus as a result of their reflections; as individuals, they examine their practices and the practices of other journalists and often reach very different conclusions.

The news coverage of a military conflict and the related reflexive chatter call attention to issues and problems salient to journalists. For example, prior to Operation Iraqi Freedom, considerable attention was paid in the opinion pages and journalistic dialogue to the embedded press system, concerns about press co-optation by the military and the administration, and perceived violations of journalistic ethics, including a heated debate concerning whether reporters retained their status as "neutrals" if they armed themselves or held wounded soldiers' weapons.[16]

---

The point he is making is that the press should present both the good and bad sides to anything and everything, because in the end, the truth always wins out.

[14] Schudson, *The Power of News*, p. 5.

[15] See Hardt, Hanno, "Conflicts of Interest: New Workers, Media, and Patronage Journalism," *Media Power, Professional and Policies,* 2000, pp. 209–224, for example.

[16] Two of the Geneva Conventions pertain to journalists: Protocol I (1977), Article 79, and the 4th article of the 3rd convention (1949); *Protocol I, Additional to the Geneva Conventions of 12 August 1949, and Relating to the Protection of the Victims of International Armed Conflicts,* 1977. From Article 79:

> Measures of protection for journalists: Journalists engaged in dangerous professional missions in areas of armed conflict shall be considered as civilians within the meaning of Article 50, paragraph 1. 2. They shall be protected as such under the Conventions and this Protocol, provided that they take no action adversely affecting their status as civilians, and without prejudice to the right of war correspondents accredited to the armed forces to the status provided for in Article 4 A (4) of the Third Convention. 3. They may obtain an identity card similar to the model in Annex II of this Protocol. This card, which shall be issued by the government of the State of which the journalist is a national or in whose territory he resides or in which the news medium employing him is located, shall attest to his status as a journalist.

**Reactive.** Both in planning and coverage, the press is primarily reactive. This trait is partly due to the nature of the news, as reporters are called upon to react to the changing current events. On a broader scale, the press tends to have a limited institutional memory. As Aukofer and Lawrence note: "Institutionally, the media only rarely, if ever, plan anything together. Although individual news organizations work out their own coverage, it is usually done under the gun, at the last minute."[17] They continue: "The competitive and independent nature of the news media is such that, with rare exceptions, they cannot organize and plan in a way that represents all of their constituent parts."[18]

Even in the focus of its stories, the press follows more than it leads. To gain market share, the press often follows the tides of public opinion. For example, Schudson convincingly asserts that the press was more reactive than proactive as far as the changing tide of public opinion was concerned in Vietnam.[19]

Technological developments facilitate the press's reactive nature. The wide availability of cable or satellite television, together with im-

---

From the 4th article of the 3rd convention:

> (4) Persons who accompany the armed forces without actually being members thereof, such as civilian members of military aircraft crews, war correspondents, supply con tractors, members of labour units or of services responsible for the welfare of the armed forces, provided that they have received authorization, from the armed forces which they accompany, who shall provide them for that purpose with an identity card similar to the annexed model.

These conventions abut journalistic ethics to the extent that if some reporters choose not to adhere to Geneva Convention guidelines for their own maintenance of noncombatant status, those reporters threaten the ability of other reporters to do so, not before the law, but as a practical matter.

[17] Aukofer, Frank, and William P. Lawrence, *America's Team, the Odd Couple: A Report on the Relationship Between the Media and the Military*, Nashville, Tenn.: Freedom Forum First Amendment Center at Vanderbilt University, 1995, p. 1.

[18] Aukofer and Lawrence, *America's Team*, p. 7.

[19] Schudson, *The Power of News*, pp. 22–23; Hallin, Daniel C., "The Media, the War in Vietnam, and Political Support: A Critique of the Thesis of an Oppositional Media," *The Journal of Politics*, Vol. 46, No. 1, February 1984, pp. 2–24; and Bennett, W. Lance, "Toward a Theory of Press-State Relations in the United States," *Journal of Communication*, Vol. 40, No. 2, Spring 1990, pp. 103–125, also concur.

provements in communication technology (satellite phones and uplinks, "lipstick" cameras, etc.), allows news to be broadcast continuously, and often raw or live. This creates a 24-hour news cycle, where the copy deadline is "now."[20] The demands of this 24-hour news cycle can inhibit verification of stories.[21] "Journalism is becoming less a product than a process, witnessed in real time and in public."[22]

**Professional.** Professionalism is a means of injecting credibility and reliability into reporting. "Journalists see themselves as professionals rather than partisans. They act to uphold professional tenets rather than to satisfy political passions."[23]

Although professionalism involves aspirations to a professional code of conduct and journalistic ethics, disagreement exists concerning what constitutes the precise standards of professionalism, since standards have not been codified. Schudson argues that journalistic professionalism can pull news reporting in four directions: news is generally negative, presented in a detached manner, technical, and "official."[24]

### Press Goals for News Coverage

We now turn to a discussion of the press's goals for news coverage, particularly as they are relevant to wartime news and military-press relations. Because the press's business *is* news, the press's goals for

---

[20] Gowing, Nik, *Real-Time Television Coverage of Armed Conflicts and Diplomatic Crises: Does It Pressure or Distort Foreign Policy Decisions?* Cambridge, Mass.: Joan Shorenstein Barone Center on the Press Politics and Public Policy John F. Kennedy School of Government Harvard University, 1994; Livingston, Stephen, *Clarifying the CNN Effect: An Examination of Media Effects According to Type of Military Intervention,* Cambridge, Mass.: Joan Shorenstein Center of the John F. Kennedy School of Government, Harvard University, Research Paper R-18, 1997.

[21] Tumber, Howard, "Democracy in the Information Age: The Role of the Fourth Estate in Cyberspace," *Information, Communication and Society,* Vol. 4, No. 1, 2001, pp. 95–112.

[22] Rosenstiel, T., and B. Kovach, "The Journalism That Doesn't Bother to Check Its Facts," *Herald Tribune,* March 3, 1999, p. 8.

[23] Schudson, *The Power of News*, p. 7.

[24] Schudson, *The Power of News*, p. 9.

news coverage are intrinsic to its core mission. The press's 4th Estate obligations and business interest in attaining profits mean that the press needs information in order to fulfill its mission. As a result, one of the press's primary goals for news coverage is to gain access to newsworthy information. Two other goals follow from the need for access. The press seeks to provide information to the public and, in doing so, seeks to maintain journalistic standards for the quality of news, including accuracy, objectivity (telling both sides of the story), and credibility.

**Gain Access to Newsworthy Information.** To get good stories, reporters need access to them. In short, access is critical for the press to achieve its mission. The press must have access to the actions of government if it is to satisfy the public's "right to know." Note that this right to know, while broadly espoused and frequently used to advocate increased press access, does not enjoy the same kind of explicit constitutional protection that the "free press" does[25]; nonetheless, if the press is to effectively serve 4th Estate functions, it certainly needs access to newsworthy government actions.[26] For a more extensive discussion of the public's right to know, see Appendix A.

As we shall see in the next chapter, access has traditionally been the biggest source of tension between the press and the military. Peter Andrews observes:

> After more than 130 years, the fundamental dispute between the American media and the American military has changed hardly at all. The essential argument is still about access. How much should the press be allowed to know and see of the conduct of battle? [27]

---

[25] In fact, the First Amendment assures only the freedom of speech and the freedom of the press. What exactly encompasses "freedom of the press" is a topic of considerable scholarly and legal debate.

[26] Gauthier, Candace Cummins, "Right to Know, Press Freedom, Public Discourse," *Journal of Mass Media Ethics,* Vol. 14, No. 4, 1999, pp. 197–212.

[27] Andrews, "The Media and the Military," p. 78.

**Provide Newsworthy Information to the Public.** The press's obligations as the 4th Estate imply both rights and responsibilities. To serve as a check on the three branches of government, the press must be allowed to report on the government. Press freedom of this kind is implicitly assured by the First Amendment. But if the press is acting to satisfy the public's right to know, then the press undertakes a duty to the public. If the public must have access to newsworthy information in order to participate in the governing process, and the 4th Estate serves the role of providing that information, then the media itself must take the responsibility to present all sides of issues so that an informed citizenry can make decisions on matters of national policy.[28]

From a business perspective, however, the goal of informing the public is related to building market share. Depending on the specific media, this interest may take the form of seeking to increase circulation or distribution, or paying attention to viewer counts or ratings.[29]

The pursuit of profit via market share shapes what is considered a newsworthy story. For example, reporters tend to pursue "good" stories, stories that grab attention for whatever reason (which leads to what Dan Rather has called the "showbizification" of news).[30] They also focus on getting "scoops" or exclusives; it is commonly understood that if one news outlet consistently has good stories and no one else has them, its market share increases.

**Maintain Quality of News.** Maintaining journalistic standards of professionalism is a goal for many reporters and news organizations. Although different views exist concerning exactly what constitutes standards of professionalism for journalists, several factors are frequently mentioned, including accuracy, objectivity, quality of investigation and reporting, and the personal integrity of the reporter.

---

[28] Baroody, Judith Raine, *Media Access and the Military: The Case of the Gulf War*, Lanham, Md.: University Press of America, 1998.

[29] Napoli, Philip M., "A Principal-Agent Approach to the Study of Media Organizations: Toward a Theory of the Media Firm," *Political Communication*, No. 14, Vol. 2, 1997, p. 207.

[30] Quoted in Schudson, *The Power of News*, p. 6.

Schudson has identified several components of quality journalism, including "full and fair information," "coherent frameworks to help citizens comprehend the complex political universe," and "a forum for dialogue among citizens that not only informs democratic decision making but is an element in it."[31]

The profit motive and the pressures it creates to build market share can come into tension with other press goals for news coverage, particularly those relating to the quality of information. Often individual reporters can be more concerned with the professionalism and credibility displayed in their writing than with profit. For example, a print journalist we interviewed talked about *his* credibility and integrity, and *his* duty to his readers.

Indeed, the quality of news is intrinsically tied to the reporter's own credibility. *Baltimore Sun* editor James Houck said, "The most valuable asset a paper has is its credibility. If people think we don't cover stories because they involve us, people will wonder what else we don't cover."[32] While the assertion of credibility as a "valuable asset" logically ties credibility to the profit motive, credibility is a press goal independent of profit motive; it is inherently tied into the nature of reporting as a valuable enterprise. Be it in service of 4th Estate goals, journalistic professionalism, or for its own sake, credibility *is* a valuable journalistic asset, and its increment and maintenance are goals pursued by the press.

## The Military

We now turn to a discussion of the military, focusing on its mission and mission-related goals, organizational characteristics, and goals for news coverage.

---

[31] Schudson, *The Power of News*, pp. 28–29.

[32] As quoted in Schudson, *The Power of News*, p. 5.

### Mission Focus: Protection and Defense of the United States

The primary mission of the military is to protect and defend the United States. While the military has other goals and obligations and is even coming to recognize the importance and value of good public relations, soldiers are inclined by nature to give lesser priority to anything that isn't the primary military mission.[33]

The military achieves its overarching mission through the success of individual military operations. Operational success depends in large part on operational security, which, as will be discussed below, is critically important in determining the military's goals regarding news coverage during operations.

### Institutional Characteristics

We will now discuss the institutional characteristics of the military. While doing so, we will highlight relevant comparisons to the press.

One point that merits note up front is that, in a sense, the U.S. military is monolithic in a way that the U.S. press is not. While, like the press, the military is a collection of individuals with often diverse views and values, in some very real sense all members of the military ostensibly pursue the same goals and are all part of the same command hierarchy, ultimately culminating in the national command authority. The common purpose and unified command behind the military lead to some institutional characteristics that are very different from those found among the more heterogeneous press.

**Hierarchical/Cooperative.** The military is hierarchically organized in strict chains of command, culminating with the commander in chief. While there are rivalries among the services and among different units, military efforts are fundamentally cooperative and focused on the primary mission. Common goals are pursued in an organized, integrated fashion. The strict military hierarchy stands in contrast to the more horizontally organized press, in which different media outlets compete directly and fiercely for market share.

---

[33] Aukofer and Lawrence, *America's Team.*

Where there is competition within the military, it is usually at the highest levels of aggregation: rivalries among the services for "credit" or prestige for their (comparative) accomplishments. For example, from an airman's perspective, U.S. victory is the goal, but if the Air Force makes the largest contribution to that victory, even better.[34]

Along with hierarchy, there is obedience to the command structure. Soldiers follow the orders they are given, except under rare and exceptional circumstances. This is particularly important because if someone at the top of the hierarchy makes a clear and unambiguous decision and orders specific action on that decision down the chain of command, it is very likely that that decision will be realized, as will be apparent in the discussion of several of the case studies included in the next chapter.

However, when orders are *not* clear and singular, the diverse natural impulses of individuals may take over. As reporter Tom DeFrank notes about incentives and conflicting instructions for military officers:

> And the other factor is, as my four-star general friend says—and as you alluded to it earlier—if my job is to do my mission and I get somewhat conflicting advice—one from an assistant secretary of events or public affairs saying let's have as much access as we can, and a three-star general saying, I don't want those people around here—who do you think I'm going to listen to? The ASDPA [Assistant Secretary of Defense for Public Affairs] or somebody who writes my next efficiency report? I don't think—I mean, I don't ascribe ill motives to this. I think there's a lot of good faith and a lot of goodwill on both sides here, but I

[34] Consider, for example, the competition among the services during OIF for positive media attention as documented in Cooper, Christopher, and David Cloud, "Branches of U.S. Military Fight over Media Attention in Iraq: Armed Services Compete over Air Time and Credit; A Final Battle over Budgets?" *Wall Street Journal*, March 26, 2003.

> do think there is this fundamental issue, and I don't think it is going to get fixed.[35]

**Reflexive.** Like the press, the military is reflexive, but in a different way. The military is what we call "constructively reflexive." Unlike the uncoordinated process of press reflexivity, in which individual reporters share their views in the news, military reflexivity is embodied in formal "lessons learned" processes. Military action generates "after action reports," which can be used for formal lessons learned activities or for other forms of evaluation. The military actively seeks out evidence of shortcomings and attempts to analyze and redress them.

**Proactive and Reactive.** Unlike the press, the military has a strong institutional memory. Given that "generals always fight the last war," it is unsurprising that the military, after reflexive evaluation, plans and institutes changes for "next time."[36] Because the military has formal evaluation procedures, it can take proactive steps for the future based on the lessons learned. In contrast, the press has very limited ability to plan ahead cohesively or at all far in advance; this is not surprising given the many diverse news outlets and organizations that constitute the press.

It is important to keep in mind that the military's proactive learning process isn't perfect. The military occasionally "forgets" lessons from past wars, or learns the "wrong" lesson from time to time. Nonetheless, the point of note is that the military is formally proactive in its planning. Moreover, the military is also reactive in certain respects. Indeed, flexibility in response both in and out of combat is an important military attribute.

---

[35] Tom DeFrank, *New York Daily News,* quoted in Clarke, Victoria (presenter), *Seminar on Coverage of the War on Terrorism,* News Transcript, Washington, D.C.: U.S. Department of Defense and The Brookings Institution, November 8, 2001. Online at http://www.defenselink.mil/news/Nov2001/t11182001_t1108br.html (as of September 17, 2003).

[36] See Chapter 4 in Paul, Christopher, *Marines on the Beach: How the U.S. Arrives at Armed Intervention*, Dissertation, Los Angeles: University of California at Los Angeles, 2001, for a discussion.

**Professional.** The current U.S. military is highly professional. The all-volunteer force has come to be defined by its high levels of skill, dedication, and discipline.[37] In the years since Vietnam, the military has gone to great lengths to improve the quality and reputation of its troops. King and Karabell describe the "3 P's" of the military: performance, professionalism, and persuasion.[38]

The military's emphasis on professionalism provides a point of commonality with the press, although what it means to be a professional reporter and what it means to be a professional soldier are very different things. Nonetheless, both institutions have developed traditions and standards. Because the professional standards developed by each institution originate at least partly in response to cultural and historical needs, they can be viewed, to a certain extent, as products more of history and culture than of anything inherent to the job of reporting or soldiering.[39]

### Military Goals Related to News Coverage

While the press's goals for news coverage are intrinsic to its main mission of reporting, the military's goals for news are separate from and largely subordinate to its mission-related goals of operational success and security. As will be apparent in the discussion that follows, many of the military's goals with regard to news coverage grow out of the tension between its mission-related goals (achieve operational success and maintain operational security) and those of the press (especially the goals of gaining access to information and providing information to the public). At the same time, the military has its own goals for using news coverage in a way that supports its military mission.

**Do Not Allow News Coverage to Compromise Operational Success or Security.** Operational security is the goal most proximate to the military's capital "G" goal of mission success. The press's interest

---

[37] King, David C., and Zachary Karabell, *The Generation of Trust: How the U.S. Military Has Regained the Public's Confidence Since Vietnam*, Washington, D.C.: The AEI Press, 2003.

[38] King and Karabell, *The Generation of Trust.*

[39] Schudson, *The Power of News.*

in gaining access to and releasing newsworthy information to the public can potentially threaten the success of a military mission. If mission details are made available to the enemy prior to or even during an operation, operational security has been compromised, and the mission may be jeopardized. "At the core, if it comes down to operational security or press access, you're exactly right: military officers will always choose operational security."[40]

The military's chief goal with regard to news coverage is thus to ensure that news coverage pertaining to the military mission does not compromise the success of that mission. This goal acknowledges the importance of the press's own obligations but gives priority to the success of the military endeavor.

The need to ensure operational security can come into conflict with other military goals related to news coverage. For example, although the military has come to appreciate the value of good public relations and the necessity of engaging the press (discussed below), such objectives can come into conflict with operational security concerns.

**Fulfill Legal Obligations in Regard to Press Access.** The military's second goal with regard to news coverage is also related to the differing missions and obligations of the military and the press. The Constitution allows for the military to provide for the common defense, and every military officer takes an oath to uphold the Constitution. While the military mission is the first priority, that mission can never be at the expense of the laws and the Constitution. Military legal obligations include accountability to the civilian leadership and protection of the Constitution, including the First Amendment. Press coverage of military operations allows confirmation that the military is acting in accordance with American values and laws.

The military's precise legal obligations regarding press access and the public's right to know[41] are unclear, however; and the different

---

[40] Rear Admiral Steven Pietropaoli (Chief of Information, U.S. Navy) quoted in Clarke, *Seminar on Coverage of the War on Terrorism,* p. 19.

[41] See Appendix A for an extensive discussion of the public's right to know.

views of the military and the press on this matter can sometimes lead to legal dispute. But, while it seems likely that the military could *in practice* get away with extensive press exclusions in the name of operational security, *in principle* the military considers the satisfaction of legal and constitutional obligations through press access to be an important goal.[42]

**Use News Coverage to Support Military Mission.** While the first two goals for news coverage focus on potential constraints on the free flow of information in order to safeguard the operational success and security of military operations, the military also recognizes that news coverage can play a positive role in military success. Indeed, the military has come to accept news coverage as not only an obligation, but a desired goal in its own right.

> Media coverage of any future operation will, to a large extent, shape public perception of the national security environment now and in the years ahead. This holds true for the U.S. public; the public in allied countries whose opinion can affect the durability of our coalition; and publics in countries where we conduct operations, whose perceptions of us can affect the cost and duration of our involvement. Our ultimate strategic success in bringing peace and security to this region will come in our long-term commitment to supporting our democratic ideals. We need to tell the factual story—good or bad—before others seed the media with disinformation and distortions, as they most certainly will continue to do.[43]

The military seeks to use news coverage to support its military mission in three main ways: by supporting positive public relations

---

[42] It should be noted that embedding the press with troops is *not* a constitutional right. See Kirkland, Michael, "No 'Right' for Media to Embed with Troops," *Washington Times*, February 4, 2004, who notes that part of the court's findings in rejecting a suit brought by Larry Flint over access in Afghanistan asserted that "there is no constitutional right for the media to embed with U.S. military forces in combat."

[43] Secretary of Defense, Office of Assistant Secretary of Defense, Public Affairs, *Public Affairs Guidance (PAG) on Embedding Media During Possible Future Operations/Deployments in the U.S. Central Commands (CENTCOM) Area of Responsibility,* cable to various military and government offices, February 10, 2003.

and building public support; by building credibility; and by supporting successful information operations against the enemy. Each is discussed briefly below.

**Obtain Positive Public Relations/Build Public Support.** One of the oft-repeated "lessons" of Vietnam is that the military cannot wage a war without domestic public support. Whether or not this statement is "true" in all circumstances, clearly there are advantages accruing to morale and political support from public support.[44] Positive public relations are important for building public support.

Given the military's current commitment to the 3 P's[45] (performance, professionalism, and persuasion), the military has "an overriding self-interest in getting its overwhelmingly positive story out."[46] If the military can effectively convey its performance and professionalism, it can persuade the public to support it.

The kind of public relations the military receives for a particular operation often depends on the level of access provided to the press. For example, when the military denies access to its operations, the press often responds by focusing its stories on the denial of access itself. Aukofer and Lawrence observe that coverage of the Grenada intervention in 1983, in which the press was completely excluded for the first 48 hours, consisted mostly of press complaints about denial of access, with much less attention paid to the actual conflict.[47] The press will complain if it feels that it is not able to fulfill its 4th Estate function or that the military is being unreasonable in preventing the press from witnessing events that fall within the scope of the public right to know. Moreover, even if press access is subsequently permitted, the balance of coverage is likely to continue to be less favorable to the military, adversely affecting military public relations.

---

[44] Adamson, William G., *The Effects of Real-Time News Coverage on Military Decision-Making,* Maxwell Air Force Base, Ala.: Air Command and Staff College, 1997.

[45] King and Karabell, *The Generation of Trust.*

[46] Aukofer and Lawrence, *America's Team,* p. 5.

[47] Aukofer and Lawrence, *America's Team.*

**Build Credibility.** To develop good public relations, the military's message must be credible. This goes beyond simply being professional and performing; credibility has everything to do with *how* that activity is evidenced and presented. Secrecy can damage credibility.[48] Moreover, when the military serves as the sole source of information, it can damage its credibility as well, by leaving the press and the public to speculate about what the military *isn't* telling them.

A variety of credibility-enhancing strategies are available to the military, including allowing press access, indicating the degree of certainty attached to its reports, and admitting failures and errors prior to being accused of them.

**Support Information Operations.** Another way in which the military can use news coverage to support its military mission is by using the press to counter enemy disinformation or propaganda campaigns.[49] If a credible press is available to discredit enemy disinformation, the military is well-served.

Further, "many military leaders have become aware that news media coverage of their operations can be a force multiplier."[50] As with the recent "shock and awe" campaign accompanying the opening of the war in Iraq, coverage that demonstrates the performance and professionalism of the U.S. military to citizens at home also demonstrates those intimidating qualities to the enemy. Some researchers suggest that press coverage can be used for more extensive "information operations," but these would need to be balanced with goals for credibility and positive press relations.[51]

---

[48] Baroody, *Media Access and the Military.*

[49] See Chapter 1 in Baroody, *Media Access and the Military*.

[50] Aukofer and Lawrence, *America's Team*, p. 4.

[51] For example, see MacArthur and Bagdikian, *Second Front.*

## Comparison of the Press and the Military

> While there is—or should be—a natural convergence of interests in providing to the public accurate information about our armed forces and what they do, there is at the same time an inherent clash of interests (especially acute when men are fighting and dying) between military leaders responsible for success in battle and for the lives of their commands, and a media intensely competitive in providing readers and viewers with quick and vivid "news" and opinion.[52]

The press and the military do indeed have very different natures and goals, and these differences have historically resulted in tension and seem likely to continue to do so in the future. Table 2.1 summarizes and contrasts the differences between the press and the military in terms of each institution's mission, characteristics, and goals for news coverage.

A review of the discussion to this point allows us to make several observations about the relationship between the military and the press. First, the main mission of the press is an information-related mission while that of the military is not. This point may seem obvious, but it is an important one because these different missions can come into conflict, particularly during military operations.

However, while the missions of the military and the press clearly differ, each institution must also resolve tensions within itself as it pursues a range of competing concerns and goals, particularly with regard to news coverage. These diverse concerns and goals can modify the way in which each institution pursues its main mission. For example, the military's interest in using news coverage to support its mission might result in more press access than would a focus on maintaining operational security alone. Along a different line, the press's interest in increasing market share might in some instances threaten the sincerity of its pursuit of 4th Estate obligations.

---

[52] General Andrew J. Goodpaster (U.S. Army, ret.) quoted in Belknap, Margaret H., "The CNN Effect: Strategic Enabler or Operational Risk?" *Parameters,* Vol. 32, No. 3, Autumn 2002, p. 101.

**Table 2.1**
**Comparison of Press and Military Missions and Goals**

| Press | Military |
|---|---|
| | **Mission** |
| Reporting | Protection and defense of the United States |
| | **Mission-Related Goals** |
| Uphold obligations to the public<br>Achieve profits | Achieve operational success<br>Maintain operational security |
| | **Organizational Attributes** |
| Horizontal/competitive<br>Reflexive<br>Reactive<br>Professional | Hierarchical/cooperative<br>Reflexive<br>Reactive and Proactive<br>Professional |
| | **Goals for News Coverage** |
| Gain access to newsworthy information<br>Provide newsworthy information to the public<br>Fulfill obligations to the public<br>Build market share<br>Maintain quality of news<br>Objectivity (tell both sides of the story)<br>Accuracy<br>Credibility | Do not allow news coverage to compromise operational security<br>Fulfill legal obligations regarding press access<br>Use news coverage to support military mission<br>Obtain good public relations<br>Build credibility<br>Support information operations |

Another observation to be made about the relationship of the military and the press concerns the critical role played by *access* within military-press relations. Press access forms the foundation on which the press can fulfill its other two goals for news. Simply put, without some form of access, there is no story to report. While access is critical to the press's mission, it is also pivotal with regard to the military's mission as well since the need to ensure operational security can come into conflict with the press's goal of access. Attempts by the military to deny access are often the result of basic conflicts between the institutions' respective missions. From the military's perspective, the security concerns of any particular operation are more important than the need for immediate press access. From the press's perspective, the denial of access in some situations might be viewed instead as an attempt by the military to impede the press from fulfilling its basic mission and from exercising its First Amendment rights.

But military concerns about access should not overshadow the fact that, over the past several decades, there has been a growing military recognition of the importance—and the inevitability—of news coverage. In the contemporary era, the military has come to accept the necessity of press coverage (and its role in informing citizens) and to realize the advantages that can come from positive press coverage. This realization of the importance of press coverage has even played a role in situations when the military has tried to limit access, as in the first Gulf War, where the military tried to be the main source of combat footage. One result of the military's recognition of the importance of news coverage has been the use of more sophisticated public relations efforts.

Moreover, while the press and the military seem to be different in respect to many characteristics and goals, there are also many commonalities, and these elements of common ground may ultimately provide important areas of overlap from the perspective of each institution in evaluating the "success" of various instances of press-military relations. The two most prominent areas of overlap are the emphasis placed by both institutions on professionalism and the importance for both of serving the public and upholding the Constitution, even if these are achieved in very different ways.

## Goals of the Press or Military Vis-à-Vis the Public

In this section, we consider the goals of the press and the military with regard to the public. Both the press and the military seek to serve the public's interests.

> All concerned recognize, at least in theory, that media scrutiny is an aspect of a healthy civilian control of the military and also an

> exercise of free speech—both cornerstones of the Constitution, which military people are sworn to uphold.[53]

### The Public's Goals for News Coverage

But how does the public benefit from war coverage? In this subsection, we consider two main goals on the part of the public regarding news coverage. First is the goal of getting information and interpretation. Second is the notion of having the information necessary to function in a democracy, that is, to be "well-served" by news coverage.

**Get Information and Interpretation.** Fundamentally, during war citizens rely heavily on the media for information and interpretation.[54]

> In serving the purposes of the American public abroad, the military is supposed to operate consistently with American values. The press serves as the representative of the American public in monitoring both the military and the government and in making sure that those institutions function in the best interests of the public. In order to effectively perform this role, the press needs access to U.S. combat operations and the freedom to publish without military oversight except in the case of legitimate security concerns.[55]

Whether or not each news agency chooses to fulfill its duty to act as the 4th Estate, the public writ large is relying on the press (also writ large) to do so.

**Seek to Be "Well-Served."** Although there is consensus that the free press *has* an important role in democracy, there is wide-ranging debate on what *exactly* the role of a free press in democracy is.[56] In

---

[53] Porch, "No Bad Stories," p. 6.

[54] Baroody, *Media Access and the Military.*

[55] Steger, "Slicing the Gordian Knot," p. 1007.

[56] See for example Gauthier, "Right to Know, Press Freedom, Public Discourse"; Baroody, *Media Access and the Military*; Tumber, "Democracy in the Information Age"; Gans, Herbert

other words, how does a free press serve society *well* in a democracy? Various theories differ on *how* the press's role serves democracy. Some theories are prospective and maintain that the role of the press is to inform the public of *what is happening now*, with the understanding that informed citizens are both more likely to participate politically and are better participants. Other theories are retrospective and focus on the role of the press as "witness" to what *has happened*, thereby allowing citizens to evaluate the actions of government and, if necessary, to seek to change their representatives in the next electoral cycle.

## Press-Military Relations

The press's role in serving the public must also be considered in relation to the military's own public service role. Given that the military and the media both serve the public good, exactly *how* the press can best do this is open for debate. For example, the public opinion literature suggests that the public can be better "informed" as a result of *more* coverage.[57] Figure 2.1 shows that, historically, increased news coverage of military operations has made the public more aware of these issues.

Figure 2.1 plots the number of *New York Times* articles containing the name of the country in which the U.S. military was involved in a week in which the Roper poll asked its "following the issue" question versus the percentage of Roper poll respondents who reported following the issue. Each data point represents a week that a Roper poll was conducted. For that week, a data point shows the number of *New York Times* articles (horizontal axis) versus the percentage of Roper poll respondents indicating that they were "following the issue" (vertical axis). Clearly, coverage of and attention to an

J., "What Can Journalists Actually Do for American Democracy?" *Press/Politics,* Vol. 3, No. 4, 1998, pp. 6–12.

[57] McCombs, Maxwell E., and Donald L. Shaw, "The Agenda Setting Function of Mass Media," *Public Opinion Quarterly,* Vol. 36, No. 2, Summer 1972, pp. 176–187; Price, Vincent, and John Zaller, "Who Gets the News? Alternative Measures of News Reception and Their Implications for Research," *Public Opinion Quarterly,* Vol. 57, No. 2, Summer 1993, pp. 133–164.

**Figure 2.1**
**Those in the Public Following a Particular Issue Versus the Number of Articles Mentioning a Country in Which the U.S. Military Was Involved**

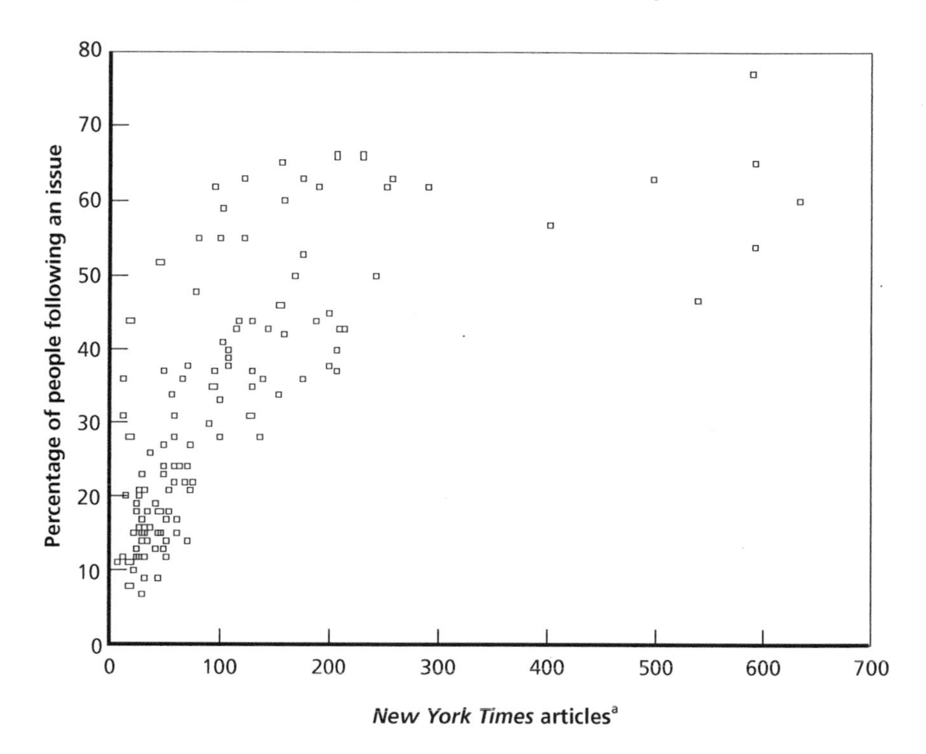


SOURCES: The Roper Center for Public Opinion Research (www.ropercenter.uconn.edu), Times Mirror (www.timesmirrorfoundation.org), Princeton Survey Research Associates (www.psra.com), The Gallup Organization (www.gallup.com), *The New York Times* (www.nytimes.com), CBS (www.cbsnews.com/sections/opinion/polls/main 500160.shtml), CNN (www.cnn.com), *USA Today*/CNN/Gallup (http://www.usatoday.com/news/polldex.htm, The Pew Research Center for the People and the Press (www.people-press.org), the *Los Angeles Times* (http://www.latimes.com/news/custom/timespoll/), NBC (www.nbc.com), ABC News (abcnews.go.com), *The Wall Street Journal* (online.wsj.com/public/us), International Communications Research (www.icrsurvey.com), The Associated Press (www.ap.org), *The Washington Post* (http://www.washingtonpost.com/wp-srv/politics/polls/vault/vault.htm), *Newsweek* (www.newsweek.com), and The Henry J. Kaiser Family Foundation/Harvard Kennedy School of Government (www.kff.org)—all accessed through Lexis-Nexis Academic Universe, 1990–2003, (www.lexis-nexis.com) and unpublished data compiled by Eric Larson using New York Times Article Archive, 1990–2003, *The New York Times on the Web*, http://www.nytimes.com.

[a]Containing the name of a country (Iraq, Somalia, Haiti, and Bosnia) in which the U.S. military was involved.

**RAND** *MG200-2.1*

issue are correlated (and equally clear from the general curved shape of the point "cloud," that the relationship is either nonlinear or is affected by some other variable or variables).

From the public's point of view, where does that leave press-military relations? Some have argued that "good faith" tension between military and the press serves the public interest by keeping both sides honest.[58] This notion harks back to Jentleson's and Oneal, Lian, and Joyner's writings about the prudence of the public and the role of the media in reducing public ignorance.[59]

The public appears to acknowledge the tension between the respective missions of the press and the military, in particular regarding the conflict between reporter access and operational security. In resolving that tension, the majority seem to favor the military. As a specific example, a Pew survey showed that the

> majority of Americans (59%) believe that the military, rather than news organizations, should exert more control over news on the war in Afghanistan. That is about the same proportion that supported military censorship in the Persian Gulf War a decade ago (57%).[60]

The public wants military victory, but also wants (and arguably has a right to) news coverage of war and other military operations. The press and the military support both these objectives, though with slightly different priorities. The resulting tensions may or may not be a bad thing; most important for the achievement of the public's goals

---

[58] Hickey, "Access Denied."

[59] Jentleson, Bruce W., "The Pretty Prudent Public: Post Post-Vietnam American Opinion on the Use of Military Force," *International Studies Quarterly*, Vol. 36, No. 1, March 1992, pp. 49–73; Oneal, John R., Brad Lian, and James H. Joyner, Jr., "Are the American People 'Pretty Prudent'? Public Responses to U.S. Uses of Force, 1950–1988," *International Studies Quarterly*, Vol. 40, No. 2, June 1996, pp. 261–279.

[60] The Pew Charitable Trusts, "No Rise in Fears or Reported Depression; Public Remains Steady in Face of Anthrax Scare," *Public Opinion and Polls*, Washington, D.C.: The Pew Research Center for the People & the Press, October 15, 2001. Online at http://www.pewtrusts.com/ideas/ideas_item.cfm?content_item_id=785&content_type_id=18 (as of June 17, 2004).

is that the tension be resolved reasonably, with reasonable compromises on both sides.

> But we are not talking about a zero-sum game. The press seeks to acquire and disseminate as much relevant information as possible. The military regards information as one among many variables to use and control. Too often the issue is described simplistically as a conflict between 1st Amendment rights and national security. Both history and experience teach the error of this formulation. While it is certainly possible for a careless dispatch to jeopardize legitimate national security interests, military operations and the lives of service personnel, the documented instances of such reporting are exceedingly few. In dozens of wars and military operations this century, representatives of the press have been privy to highly classified operational details or learned or observed things which could compromise legitimate security needs. In nearly all instances, they acted with restraint and responsibility.[61]

But even though the military has come to recognize the importance of good public relations and the role the press plays in the military's public relations, tensions remain between the press and the military. These tensions are derived not only from high-level differences in missions and goals, but also at the individual level: Each military operation must be evaluated in terms of its specific security risks and its newsworthiness. All press coverage comes with risks, not just to operational security, but to reputations and individual officers' careers as a result of unfavorable coverage.[62]

---

[61] Zelnick, C. Robert, "The Press and National Security: Military Secrets and First Amendment Values," *Journal of National Security Law*, 1997, p. 22.

[62] For example, "On December 10, 1995 CBS Evening News, Dan Rather asked an Army commander in Bosnia, 'What is your greatest fear?' The commander replied, 'Saying the wrong thing to the media.'" Quoted in Moskos, Charles C., *The Media and the Military in Peace and Humanitarian Operations*, Chicago, Ill.: Robert R. McCormick Tribune Foundation, 2000, p. 13.

## Conclusion

Clear differences between the missions and goals of the press and those of the military, particularly centering around the issues of access and operational security, make historical tensions between the two unsurprising and complete avoidance of tension unlikely. However, significant overlaps, including aspirations of professionalism and core goals of public service, make cooperation a reasonable possibility.

The following chapter will explore how conflict and cooperation played out as the relations between these two actors developed over time. Through a careful historical analysis of the relations between the military and the press, we seek to explore the factors and conditions that allowed cooperation to be a more (or less) viable option than conflict between the two and that led to the development of embedded press.

CHAPTER THREE

# History of Relations Between the Press and the Military

> We don't want the truth told about things here. . . . We don't want the enemy any better informed than he is.
>
> — General William Tecumseh Sherman, 1861[1]

As many scholars have noted, the history of the relationship between the U.S. media and the military has been "rocky" to say the least.[2] We have already suggested that the different missions, characteristics, and news-related goals of these two institutions may help to explain the potential for conflict. On the other hand, we have also seen that commonalities in the areas of professionalism and a commitment to public service allow for the possibility of cooperation.

A closer examination of the history between the two institutions will show that there are critical junctures in the trajectory of their interactions over time. In this chapter, we examine several case studies that will illustrate the twists and shifts in the relationship between the military and the press. Our case histories focus mainly on military operations in the post–World War II era since these are most relevant to understanding the origins of embedded press.

---

[1] As quoted in Andrews, "The Media and the Military," p. 78.

[2] See, for example, Aukofer and Lawrence, *America's Team*, p. 5; Steger, "Slicing the Gordian Knot," p. 958; Porch, "No Bad Stories," p. 85; MacArthur and Bagdikian, *Second Front*; O'Neil, Robert M., "The Press and National Security: The Media and the Military: The Persian Gulf War and Beyond," *Journal of National Security Law*, Vol. 1, December 1997, pp. 1–20.

Our examples illustrate the ways in which the respective missions and goals of the press and the military—especially as they relate to news coverage—can come into conflict on the battlefield. But the cases will also illustrate opportunities for cooperation and collaboration, which were necessary for the development of the embedded press.

## Case Studies: The Legacies of History

Each policy event is constrained to some extent by the legacies of what has occurred before. These legacies can be particularly clear when an institution, such as the military, makes a conscious effort to apply the lessons learned from past experience. However, while legacies can influence future events, they do not predetermine a particular course of action. As we shall see, in the post–World War II period, the press and the military have managed their interactions in a variety of ways, sometimes adhering closely to the tensions and conflicts of the past, and at other times actively seeking new ways of engagement.

### Vietnam: A Critical Juncture in Press-Military Relations and a Massive Legacy of Mistrust

Vietnam left both the press and the military with a mutual lasting and bitter legacy of mistrust and skepticism, a legacy that, although modified by subsequent events, is still playing out in some respects in the contemporary era. There has been considerable debate about what exactly happened in Vietnam to leave such hostility between the press and the military. Some have argued that the real problem was the absence of a military victory. As Porch puts it:

> The strained relationship between the media and the U.S. military [in Vietnam] has nothing to do with censorship—for the simple reason that media-military relations have always been rocky, never more than in World War II. The difference between World War II and Vietnam was not the presence of censorship but the absence of victory. In other conflicts, victory has

> erased memories of a troubled relationship; after Vietnam, the media was caught up in the quest for a scapegoat.[3]

Although there may be some truth to this claim, other factors also played a significant role in evolving press-military relations, especially differing views on the appropriate role of news coverage and the appropriate amount of press access.

At the outset, news coverage in Vietnam was very different from that in any previous conflict. The press was allowed unprecedented access, due largely to the growth of television as a popular mainstream medium for prime-time news. However, the different goals of the press and the military regarding news coverage strained relations over time. While the military and the administration sought to maintain public support for the war through optimistic briefings and relatively conservative body counts, the press sought to report the "whole story" of the ongoing conflict and used its access to provide graphic televised images and vivid stories that often belied the "official" accounts. Press-military relations soured as the war became protracted and as political consensus on the U.S. role in Vietnam began to break down.[4]

The military and the administration lost credibility in the process. As public support for the war declined, press-military relations became even more strained, particularly following the Tet offensive in January 1968. Tet clearly exposed the falsehood of administration claims and pushed many reporters from skepticism to outright mistrust of the military.

The breakdown of trust ultimately became prevalent among military personnel as well. As a result of the Vietnam experience,

---

[3] Porch, "No Bad Stories," p. 85.

[4] Hallin, "The Media, the War in Vietnam, and Political Support"; Kinnard, Douglas, "Vietnam Reconsidered: An Attitudinal Survey of U.S. Army General Officers," *Public Opinion Quarterly,* Vol. 39, No. 4, Winter 1975, pp. 445–456.

journalists distrusted military officials while the military viewed the press as subversive and unpatriotic.[5]

> The press, at first a faithful medium for the administration's military message, broke stories of American atrocities, fragging in the military, and inflated body counts, and labeled the daily Saigon briefings the "Five O'clock Follies."[6]

The military, in turn, experienced a fundamental change in the way it dealt with the news media.[7] In terms of its own mission, the military learned the value of keeping military engagements short and having a clear set of attainable objectives. In terms of its goals for news coverage, the military learned the value of keeping the media controlled during the opening days of the engagement and becoming the main (if not the only) source of information during times of war—in other words, of maintaining much greater control of press access.[8] The legacy of Vietnam affected not only military-press relations, but White House–press relations as well. After Vietnam, the press was much more inclined to be skeptical about administration claims in all policy areas. "Investigative journalism" became commonplace and played an important role in scandals such as Watergate.

---

[5] Gardner, Lloyd, "America's War in Vietnam: The End of Exceptionalism?" in D. Michael Shafer, ed., *The Legacy: The Vietnam War in the American Imagination*, Boston, Mass.: Beacon, 1990, p. 21.

[6] Tischler, Barbara, "Promise and Paradox: The 1960's and American Optimism" in D. Michael Shafer, ed., *The Legacy: The Vietnam War in the American Imagination*, Boston, Mass.: Beacon, 1990, p. 47.

[7] "Media vs. Military," *Common Ground*, interview with Warren Strobel, program 9828, aired July 14, 1998. Online at http://www.commongroundradio.org/shows/98/9828.html (as of June 17, 2004).

[8] Bagdikian, Ben H., "Foreword," in MacArthur and Bagdikian, *Second Front*; Steger, "Slicing the Gordian Knot"; Paul, *Marines on the Beach;* Knightley, Phillip, *The First Casualty: From the Crimea to Vietnam: The War Correspondent As Hero, Propagandist, and Myth Maker*, Bexleyheath, U.K.: Harcourt Press, 1975.

### Grenada: Backlash Against the Press

The legacy of press relations during the Vietnam era carried over into the 1980s when U.S. forces launched Operation Urgent Fury on October 25, 1983, with the stated purpose of protecting American lives on the island of Grenada after a leftist coup. The military's press policy in Grenada was a product of the legacy left by Vietnam. The top military officers involved had mostly been junior officers during the Vietnam War. As such, these individuals had a strong dislike for the press and declined to take press coverage into consideration at the planning stage of the operation.[9]

The military's official policy on press access was highly exclusionary. From the initial stages of the operation, the commanding officer of the task force, Vice Admiral Joseph Metcalf, requested that no reporters be present during the invasion in order to ensure operational security and the personal safety of the reporters. The request was supported all the way up the chain of command, including the president. The administration's justification for these restrictions mentioned the need for protection against information leakage as well as the difficulty of implementing the pool system.[10] When about 600 reporters arrived in Barbados, the military declared that allowing press access to the theater was unreasonable given that there was no prior planning for such measures.[11] No reporters were allowed to accompany the troops when the Marines landed in Grenada, and this restriction remained in force for 48 hours, at which point a pool of 15 reporters was escorted by the military onto the island. The number of reporters was increased each day until the fifth day after the invasion, when the press was given free access.[12] By this point, however, the fighting was long over, having been concluded within the first 48 hours of the operation. In developing its press policy, the military might have been following the lead of the British. Moskos

---

[9] Aukofer and Lawrence, *America's Team,* p. 44.

[10] Steger, "Slicing the Gordian Knot," pp. 969–970.

[11] Aukofer and Lawrence, *America's Team,* p. 44.

[12] Steger, "Slicing the Gordian Knot," pp. 969–970.

suggests that "the British military's complete control over reporters during the 1982 Falklands War served as the model for [the] American military's stringent control of the media in Grenada."[13] Whatever the origin of the policy, Grenada was a manifestation of the deteriorated relations between the press and military in the aftermath of the Vietnam War and can be considered the low point in press-military relations to date.

The press reacted to the restrictions on access by accusing the administration of violating its First Amendment rights. In response, the DoD commissioned retired Major General Winant Sidle to review the military's press policy. The Sidle commission released its report in 1984, which offered several recommendations[14] and which ultimately led to the creation of the first National Media Pool in 1985. The goal of the pool was to identify a small, preselected group of reporters who could be "activated" to cover late-breaking operations or operations planned in secret. In other words, the pool system would allow some press access while safeguarding the operational security of the military operations.

### Panama: Press Pool Doesn't Work

The implementation of the National Media Pool arrangement would come under serious scrutiny in Panama.[15] Because of the Sidle com-

---

[13] Moskos, *The Media and the Military in Peace and Humanitarian Operations*, p. 23.

[14] These were as follows:

> (1) Public affairs planning for military operations should be conducted concurrently with operational planning; (2) when news media pooling provides the only feasible means of early access to an operation, planning should support the largest possible press pool, but only for the minimum length of time necessary; (3) the Secretary of Defense should study whether a list of accredited journalists or merely accredited news organizations is necessary; (4) the media should voluntarily comply with security guidelines; (5) qualified military personnel should assist journalists covering combat operations; (6) the military should provide media communications as early as feasible, provided they do not interfere with combat operations; (7) military planning should consider media transportation; (8) the military should meet regularly with media leaders to discuss mutual problems.

[15] It is important to point out that the pool arrangement was implemented first in Operation Earnest Will, which was a relatively small operation involving reflagging of Kuwaiti merchant ships in 1987–1988. This operation received rather minor coverage, and there was little controversy surrounding the DoD's press policy at the time.

mission's recommendations and the creation of the National Media Pool in 1985, there was a general understanding that a press pool would be in place to cover the operation. However, the activation of the press pool was delayed by several hours. Reporters were not allowed access to the battlefield and were instead held in a barracks, where they were treated to a lesson on Panama's history for the first several hours of the operation.[16] Several reporters who were not part of the press pool went out on their own and were more successful at gaining access to ongoing events.[17]

The problems in implementing the press pool in Panama were due mostly to logistical error, as was shown during subsequent review of the operation by a panel headed by Associated Press Pentagon correspondent Fred S. Hoffman. Local military commanders in Panama were not notified of the imminent press presence before operation execution and thus were not prepared to provide access. Hoffman's committee called for future operations to provide a more careful and adequate implementation of the National Media Pool.[18] Although restrictions on press access in Panama were largely unintended, the press pool system as implemented only furthered the rift between the press and the military.

Following the gaffe in Panama, the military was more careful to consider the place of the press in future military operations. In the immediate aftermath of the operation, then Chairman of the Joint Chiefs of Staff General Colin Powell distributed a note to major military commanders stating:

> Commanders are reminded that the media aspects of military operations are important . . . and warrant your personal attention. . . . Media coverage and pool support requirements must be planned simultaneously with operational plans and should

---

[16] Paul, *Marines on the Beach*; Venable, Barry E., "The Army and the Media," *Military Review*, January–February 2002, p. 66; Steger, "Slicing the Gordian Knot."

[17] Porch, Douglas, *Media/Military Relations in the United States*, Partnership for Democratic Governance & Security, Occasional Paper # 10, July 2001. Online at http://www.pdgs.org./main-site.htm (as of September 23, 2003).

[18] Aukofer and Lawrence, *America's Team*, p. 44.

> address all aspects of operational activity, including direct combat, medical, prisoner or war, refugee, equipment repair, refueling and rearming, civic action, and stabilization activities. Public Affairs annexes should receive command attention when formulating and reviewing all such plans.[19]

Such efforts can be attributed at least in part to the press's continued demands for access. Indeed, it is difficult to know whether the DoD would still have commissioned two separate reviews of its press policies in Grenada and Panama had the media not continued to call for more access.

### First Gulf War: Coverage But Not Access

After Panama, the military made a commitment to improve press access while still providing adequate safeguards on operational security. But the resulting system of press access was also designed to respond to the continuing legacy of Vietnam, in particular to concerns about access on the part of high-level decisionmakers such as Secretary of Defense Richard Cheney and Commanding General Norman Schwarzkopf. As Steger points out, many decisions about press access during the first Gulf War "stemmed from the beliefs of Secretary Cheney and some military commanders that the press was irresponsible and had to be controlled."[20]

After months of negotiations, both the major media executives and the Pentagon agreed to a system of accreditation, press pools, and military escorts for the pending war with Iraq.[21] But although the agreement called for the press pool system to give way to more independent coverage once the initial stages of the operation were under way, press pools would become the norm for the duration of the conflict. Moreover, the military reserved for itself the right to review and

---

[19] Quoted in Aukofer and Lawrence, *America's Team*, p. 45.

[20] Steger, "Slicing the Gordian Knot," p. 974.

[21] Steger, "Slicing the Gordian Knot," p. 973.

potentially censor all printed reports before they were sent back to news agencies in the United States.[22]

Over the span of the conflict, some 1,600 reporters were in Saudi Arabia. Of these, 186 were accredited to be in escorted pools with fighting units.[23] Participants claimed, and a careful review concurred, that the press pool system was limiting and inconvenient, and that it resulted in unacceptable delays in reporting important developing events. Moreover, the military imposed several news blackouts during various phases of the war.[24] Several frustrated reporters took it upon themselves to sidestep military controls and venture unilaterally out into the frontlines, sometimes at risk to their lives.[25]

In general, however, the military was successful in implementing some of the most extensive controls ever on information and press coverage, and the public appears to have been largely indifferent to, if not entirely satisfied with, the performance of the press and the military in keeping the public informed. Gallup poll data from 1991 on the public's perception of media coverage of the war indicated that, for the period January 17–20, 1991, approximately 63 percent of the public viewed the media as having provided "excellent" coverage of the war, and about 89 percent felt coverage was "good" or "excellent"

---

[22] MacArthur and Bagdikian, *Second Front*.

[23] Steger (1994) reports that there were 192 accredited reporters for the press pool. This discrepancy may be due to the fact that he includes technical support staff while Porch (2001) does not. Steger, "Slicing the Gordian Knot," and Porch, *Media/Military Relations in the United States*.

[24] Steger, "Slicing the Gordian Knot," pp. 976–977.

[25] CBS reporter Bob Simon and several camera crew members were captured by Iraqi soldiers when they ventured outside of the pool system. CNN reporters like Peter Arnett were actually in Baghdad at the time of the first wave of allied bombing.

during this period.[26] For the period January 30–February 2, 1991, 79 percent indicated that the coverage was "good" or "excellent."[27]

Public satisfaction with press coverage can be largely attributed to the increasing media savvy of the military leadership, who were able to successfully use news coverage to enhance the military's image and win public support for its operations. As Goebel points out:

> Schwarzkopf himself was a master at these briefings. He carefully analyzed the importance of the briefings and prepared himself mentally. He wrote that after he arrived in Saudi Arabia he felt it was crucial not to "repeat the mistake we made in Grenada, where the military had stonewalled." He established four media ground rules. First, "don't let the media intimidate you." Second, "There's no law that says you have to answer all their questions." Third, "Don't answer any question that in your judgment would help the enemy." Fourth, "Don't ever lie to the American people." Thus, when Schwarzkopf gave his final briefing it made a powerful impact because of the credibility he had built up before and during the conflict by not overreporting or overpromising.[28]

The military also provided the press with spectacular combat footage. Few Americans will forget the dramatic footage from the nose cameras of precision-guided munitions as they streaked toward their targets.

But while this official footage satisfied much of the public's desire to "see" the war, the press chafed at its inability to collect its own quality footage or otherwise independently verify the information

---

[26] Gallup poll conducted January 19–20, 1991, n = 1,019, Roper Center at University of Connecticut, *Public Opinion Online*, accessed through Lexis-Nexis (as of July 27, 2004). All sources accessed through Lexis-Nexis can be viewed on the web but require a user ID and password for access.

[27] Gallup poll conducted January 30–February 2, 1991, n = 1,005, Roper Center at University of Connecticut, *Public Opinion Online*, accessed through Lexis-Nexis (as of July 27, 2004).

[28] Goebel, Douglas J., "Military-Media Relations: The Future Media Environment and Its Influence on Military Operations," Maxwell, Ala.: Air University and Air War College, 1997, p. 22.

provided by the military. The press challenged restrictions on access both during and after the war. While military operations were still under way, *Nation Magazine* joined other media outlets and individual journalists in filing formal charges to challenge the constitutionality of the DoD restrictions on the press's First Amendment rights.[29] A similar case was filed by JB Pictures. Although both cases were decided in favor of the DoD, some important rulings on merit for *Nation Magazine* gave legitimacy to the press's concerns about restrictions on media access.[30] In particular, the ruling suggested that the press had "at least some minimal right of access" to combat operations:

> If the reasoning of the recent access cases were followed in a military context, there is support for the proposition that the press has at least some minimal right of access to view and report about major events that affect the functioning of government, including, for example, an overt combat operation. As such, the government could not wholly exclude the press from a land area where a war is occurring that involves this country.[31]

Following the war, the press and the military came to a new agreement on wartime press coverage. This occurred after executives from major news organizations (i.e., *Time, Newsweek,* The Associated Press, *The Washington Post, The New York Times, Los Angeles Times, The Wall Street Journal,* and *Chicago Tribune*) petitioned the DoD. Among the media executives' demands were limitations on the use of pools to the first 24 to 36 hours of deployment, access to all major military units, no prior review of stories, and no military escorts. After nearly eight months of discussion, the two sides were able to come to agreement on all issues except that of security review.[32] The final

---

[29] See *Nation Magazine v. DoD,* 762 F. Supp. 1558; *JB Pictures Inc. v. DoD,* 86 F. 3d 236.

[30] O'Neil, "The Press and National Security," pp. 5–6.

[31] *Nation Magazine,* 752 F.2d 1572.

[32] Combelles-Siegel, Pascale, *The Troubled Path to the Pentagon's Rules on Media Access to the Battlefield, Grenada to Today,* Carlisle Barracks, Pa.: U.S. Army War College Strategic Studies Institute, 1996, p. 5.

product was a formal DoD *Principles for News Media Coverage of DoD Operations* for guiding future press coverage of all U.S. military engagements.[33]

### Somalia: The Press Turns the Tables

The new DoD principles, however, were not able to control all forms of press access. When 30,000 U.S. troops were deployed to Somalia on December 4, 1992, to protect distribution of food and medical supplies,[34] the media decided to take the opportunity to define its own access policy and unilaterally took up posts in the theater of operations before the military arrived.[35] The press could do this because the military cannot tightly control operations of this sort, often referred to as military operations other than war. Moreover, the operation was announced well before it actually began.[36] The Pentagon did not move to implement the press pool system and gave the press a significant amount of leeway to cover the humanitarian relief effort. However, unrestricted press access was largely not welcomed by the soldiers, particularly when the resulting coverage became more nega-

---

[33] These principles were as follows:

> (1) independent reporting will be the primary means of coverage; (2) the use of pools is not to be encouraged, but they may be necessary for early access; when used, they should be disbanded as early as possible; (3) logistical constraints may mandate the use of pools; (4) a system of credentials will be established, with expulsion for violators; the media will attempt to assign experienced reporters to combat operations; (5) reporters will have access to all major military units, excluding special operations; (6) escorts should not interfere with reporting; (7) the military is responsible for pool transportation and should attempt to give reporters rides whenever possible; (8) the military should facilitate rapid media communications; and (9) the principles will also apply to the standing DoD National Media Pool system (the Pentagon Pool).

[34] Kansteiner, Walter H., "U.S. Policy in Africa in the 1990s," in Jeremy R. Azrael and Emil A. Payin, eds., *Conference Report, U.S. and Russian Policymaking with Respect to the Use of Force*, Santa Monica, Calif.: RAND Corporation, CF-129-CRES, 1996.

[35] Moskos, *The Media and the Military in Peace and Humanitarian Operations*, p. 25.

[36] See Moskos, *The Media and the Military in Peace and Humanitarian Operations*; and Holohan, Anne, "Haiti 1990–6: Older and Younger Journalists in the Post–Cold War World," *Media, Culture & Society*, Vol. 25, No. 5, September 2003, pp. 691–709.

tive as the cost of continuing the mission increased and the peacekeepers began to engage in open conflict with local militias.[37]

### Haiti: Prelude to Cooperation

During humanitarian operations in Haiti in 1994, the press was also able to gain access prior to the military's arrival. But owing to the peaceful nature and relatively positive short-term outcomes of the operation, Haiti provided an opportunity for the press and the military to cooperate successfully and paved the way for improved future relations.

The coverage of the Haiti intervention contained an interesting instance of the press violating operational security. During President Carter's 11th-hour diplomatic mission trying to convince Haiti's military leaders to step down and allow for a peaceful intervention rather than an opposed invasion by U.S. forces, reporters observed intervention aircraft leaving their U.S. air bases and broadcast the story. The Haitian generals learned from subordinates that intervention aircraft were in the air and could have seized the delegation for hostages had they been so inclined.[38] Carter's mission was ultimately successful in that it allowed for a permissive intervention. It could be argued that the Haitian generals' awareness that the U.S. invasion force was actually on its way made the delegation's negotiations easier.

The military maintained more control over press access on the ground in Haiti than it had in Somalia; some reporters traveled with military units in a fashion presaging the full "embedded press" system. The Haiti experience was relatively more successful than Somalia given that both the press and the military had to work together to establish a set of ground rules. Reporters willingly complied with most of the military's operational security concerns and were given

---

[37] Porch, *Media/Military Relations in the United States*; Moskos, *The Media and the Military in Peace and Humanitarian Operations.*

[38] Thomas, Evan, "Under the Gun" *Newsweek*, Vol. 124, No. 14, October 3, 1994, p. 28.

sufficient latitude to write their stories as they saw fit.[39] As Holohan notes, the reporters

> recorded what was happening on the ground: what the military were doing, how the local population viewed them, the discrepancy between the articulated aims of the White House and what the troops were being told to do or not to do on the ground.[40]

**Bosnia and Kosovo: Proto–Embedded Press System**

Following on the heels of Haiti, U.S. operations in the former Yugoslavia were accompanied by more press-military cooperation, including another iteration of a proto-embedded press system. In Bosnia in 1995 the term "embedded press" was first used to describe a style of press procedures similar to those used in the days of World War II and Vietnam, although far more formal and planned. The process of "embedding" referred to a reporter being assigned to a unit, deploying with it, and living with it throughout a lengthy period of operations. For Task Force Eagle in Bosnia, the reporters were embedded for approximately a month.[41] There were 24 media organizations represented from the United States and 9 more from Britain, France, and Germany—all in all, 33 reporters were embedded in 15 different units.

In 1999, Operation Allied Force in Kosovo also used embedded reporters, although the system resulted in less access than had the previous campaign. Because the allied operation was exclusively an air campaign, news coverage was more difficult. Embedding with air units doesn't allow for the same kind of access that embedding with ground units does; while riding along in an aircraft may give a reporter a good idea *how* a bombing campaign is carried out, few of the

---

[39] Porch, *Media/Military Relations in the United States.*

[40] Holohan, "Haiti 1990–6," p. 706.

[41] Moskos, *The Media and the Military in Peace and Humanitarian Operations*, tells us that the reporters were embedded in December 1995 in Germany a week prior to deployment. After the first week, the embedded units entered Bosnia by land through Hungary. Once in Yugoslavia, the journalists remained with their units for two–three more weeks.

effects of the bombing can be witnessed from the air.[42] In addition, during the campaign the military resisted coverage because of concerns about operational security and pilot safety. A public statement by then Assistant Secretary of Defense for Public Affairs Kenneth Bacon notes that:

> a sophisticated government, such as the military in Yugoslavia, is very good at analyzing information—at figuring out what sorts of weapons we use on what sorts of targets; whether we think the weapons performed well or badly—and they take that information and use it to recalibrate their defenses.[43]

But the Pentagon's decision to limit press access to information ultimately created a perverse incentive for the reporters to find an alternative source of information—the enemy central command. Because reporters had limited access to Kosovo, they could not see "ethnic cleansing" as it took place; however, Milosevic made sure the press had access to sites of collateral damage resulting from the allied bombing campaign.[44] The result was that graphic reports and news headlines accompanied the mistaken allied bombing of a refugee convoy near Djakovica in April 1999.[45] Episodes such as this one called the moral authority of the NATO campaign into question and nearly proved disastrous.[46] Admiral James Ellis, the allied forces commander during the operation, observed:

> The enemy was much better at this than we were . . . and far more nimble. The enemy deliberately and criminally killed innocents by the thousands, but no one saw it. . . . We acciden-

---

[42] Porch, "No Bad Stories."

[43] ASDPA Kenneth Bacon quoted on *Newshour with Jim Lehrer*, April 6, 1999.

[44] Porch, "No Bad Stories."

[45] See, for example, "Civilians Are Slain in Military Attack on Kosovo Road," *The New York Times*, April 15, 1999, or "NATO Searches for Answers in Convoy Killings," *CNN Interactive*, April 15, 1999, both cited in Pounder, Gary, "Opportunity Lost: Public Affairs, Information Operations, and the Air War against Serbia," *Airpower Journal*, Vol. 14, 2000, p. 58.

[46] Porch, "No Bad Stories."

> tally killed innocents, sometimes by the dozens, and the world watched it on the evening news.[47]

The experience of Kosovo in 1999 illustrated the difficulty of preventing the press from gaining access to information in an age of technology. Even an outright denial of access on the part of the U.S. military could not keep the press from gaining access, although such restrictions might compromise the quality of the information obtained. Thus, the burden now lay with the military to determine how to proactively implement a system of press relations that maximizes operational security while providing sufficient press access to prevent damaging enemy misinformation from playing undisputed in the news.

### Afghanistan: Special Forces Are Hard to Cover

The U.S. engagement in Afghanistan (Operation Enduring Freedom) represented a noticeable decrease in press access compared with similar operations in the past. Afghanistan was the first U.S. military intervention waged against nonstate actors (Al Qaeda) and the regime that harbored them (Taliban). The restrictive press policy adopted in Afghanistan was partly the result of the nature of the operation: The engagement in Afghanistan was difficult for the press to cover simply because most of the ground elements of the campaign were special operations forces, which move rapidly and covertly over often very rugged terrain and make regular use of classified equipment or techniques, preventing reporters from covering their activities.

Reporters therefore could not see for themselves what was actually happening at the bombing sites. The press by and large did not have access to land and sea bases from which air attacks were launched on Taliban positions[48] nor were reporters allowed to be present on long-range bombing runs. They also had little or no oppor-

---

[47] Quoted in Pounder, "Opportunity Lost," p. 58.

[48] Hess, Stephen, "Pentagon Gamble Pays Off—So Far," reprinted from *Baltimore Sun*, April 7, 2003, by The Brookings Institution. Online at http://www.brookings.org/views/op-ed/hess/20030407.htm (as of September 23, 2003).

tunity to interview either pilots or special operations forces when they returned from their missions. Even the aircraft carrier *Kitty Hawk,* which served as the launch base for numerous special operations, was inaccessible to the reporters.[49]

But although reporters faced greater restrictions on access in Afghanistan, they did not make serious protests of the kind seen in previous operations. This may have been partly because of the press's interest in and concern for the events of 9/11 and other domestic issues. Nonetheless, press exclusion in this campaign was so significant that one of the top DoD officials for press affairs apologized publicly to the press for failing to make a sufficient effort to satisfy its needs. Over the long term, the military and the press will likely need to reach a compromise to resolve the conflict between the difficulty of covering certain operations (e.g., air wars and special forces campaigns) and the growing expectations for broad access and extensive news coverage.

### Major Combat Operations in Iraq: The Triumph of Embedded Press

Because Operation Iraqi Freedom was a much larger campaign than either Afghanistan or Kosovo, the issue of press access could not be avoided. The scale of the war precluded the possibility that the military could simply ignore the press, which continued to clamor for greater access. In trying to find a balance between the press's interest in gaining access and its own goals for maintaining operational security and supporting its operations through news coverage, the DoD, for the first time since Vietnam, considered a massive deployment of reporters with the troops while imposing relatively few additional constraints. But while the resulting press access arrangement was reminiscent of those used in World War II and Vietnam, it was more formalized and large scale.[50]

---

[49] Hickey, "Access Denied," p. 2.

[50] Not only were Haiti and Bosnia different types of operations (one peacekeeping, the other a joint NATO campaign), but in relation to Gulf War II, the ground components in these other campaigns were relatively smaller.

There were several factors driving the DoD to seek greater understanding and cooperation with the press. Perhaps most important was the pressure for access mounted by reporters and media organizations such as the International News Safety Institute (INSI) and the Military Reporters and Editors (MRE) group.[51] From the press's perspective, the military had failed to deliver on its promises regarding access in Kosovo and Afghanistan. Press dissatisfaction with and skepticism of the Pentagon's promises were once again on the rise.[52] In addition, advanced communications and information technology made large-scale censorship of any kind virtually impossible. Moreover, the DoD also had come to a better understanding of the importance of news coverage in supporting its own military objectives. The experience of Kosovo and Afghanistan illustrated that excluding the press from the theater can allow the adversary to use the media to wage a relatively successful propaganda campaign.

As a result, the DoD took a much more proactive approach to news coverage for the second Gulf War than it had for past operations. In spring 2001, the Pentagon brought in Victoria Clarke as Assistant Secretary of Defense for Public Affairs. Clarke's appointment coincided with the reappointment of James Wilkinson (White House

---

[51] MRE is a nonprofit organization boasting a membership of from 100 to 200 reporters that called for more "access" in future military campaigns. INSI is a Belgium-based group consisting of 80 media companies, journalists, and press freedom groups—in the ensuing days of conflict in Iraq, INSI acted as the monitor for the U.S. military's press policy.

[52] As Hickey, "Access Denied," pp. 26–31, explains, the level of access that the press received in this operation was very similar to that of Kosovo.

> First, journalists in the Afghanistan theatre did not have reasonable access to land and sea bases from which air attacks were launched on Taliban positions. Thus: no press presence on long-range bombing runs, and little or no opportunity to interview pilots upon their return from their missions. Correspondents have had no expectation of accompanying commando units into Afghanistan—an acceptable restraint, since journalists are not parachute- or combat-trained. But neither have they been permitted to interview those Special Operations forces after the fact to confirm, independently, the success or failure of missions and the extent of casualties. The aircraft carrier *Kitty Hawk*—the launch base for many of those commando raids—was off limits. Journalists had no independent contact with such units as the 10th Mountain Division while it was poised in Uzbekistan awaiting action, nor with the Marine Expeditionary Units just before they entered Afghanistan from ships in the Arabian Sea in late November, nor with other American forces in Pakistan, Tajikistan, and Oman.

Spokesman) to the U.S. Central Command as the head of strategic communications, and Bryan Whitman as Clarke's aide and Pentagon spokesperson.

The press also assembled its own group of key players, and on January 13–17, 2002, 50 bureau chiefs of major news agencies met with representatives of the DoD to discuss setting up the ground rules for an embedded press system.[53] The meeting resulted in the *Coalition Forces Land Component Command Ground Rules Agreement*, which laid out the guidelines for embedded reporters.[54] The military and the press came to agreement on other issues as well. It was understood that unit commanders might restrict the use of electronic equipment in certain tactical situations but that the Pentagon would not review or censor reporter dispatches. The DoD also reserved for itself the right to determine which reporters received the choicest "embed slots."[55] The overall objective in implementing these types of arrangements was to give reporters as much access as possible without sacrificing operational security. The success of this approach depended on a system of training and continued communication between the press and DoD public affairs.[56]

---

[53] Ricchiardi, Sherry, "Preparing for War," *American Journalism Review*, March 2003.

[54] The agreement stated that the embedded reporters are permitted to consult the unit commander before releasing information that may be sensitive; have free access to military personnel at all levels; report general information about troop strength, casualties, and captured enemy forces; report information and location of military targets and objectives previously under attack; and report names and hometowns of service members with their consent. The agreement also stated that embedded reporters are prohibited from carrying guns and/or other weapons, using personal vehicles, breaking away from the unit to conduct off-the-record interviews, taking photographs of defense installations and prisoners of war without permission, using information about casualties before their next of kin are informed, and giving details about ongoing future operations.

[55] Based on our interviews, we know that, on the whole, the 50 largest circulation media outlets with Washington bureaus were given priority for embedding.

[56] The DoD implemented a short-term crash course boot camp for reporters in places such as Quantico and Fort Benning. Brightman, Carol, "In Bed with the Pentagon," *The Nation*, March 17, 2003, indicated that only about 238 American journalists actually participated in this program. The rest either had prior experience in wartime reporting or were trained by private consultants who were hired by the respective news agencies. It is worth mentioning that all of the costs associated with training the reporters, with exception of food, were paid for by the DoD.

From the military's perspective, the benefits of embedding outweighed the costs. The military recognized that news coverage could be used to support its operational objectives. For example, one of the objectives of Operation Iraqi Freedom was to scare the enemy into submission. What better way to achieve this objective than to give Iraqis a televised view (courtesy of ABC) of the lines of 3rd Infantry Division tanks stretching beyond the horizon as they crossed into Iraq? In addition, having "an objective reporter . . . observing and being able to report in real time, as opposed to having to take the word of an Iraqi news agency or the Pentagon" would help counter the expected Anti-American propaganda.[57] Assistant Secretary of Defense for Public Affairs Clarke voiced a similar interest in using news coverage to support military objectives:

> It is in our interest to let people see for themselves through the news media, the lies and deceptive tactics Saddam Hussein will use. He will put military assets next to civilians and blame any casualties on us. It's better if the Washington Posts of the world are telling people than us.[58]

In some ways, having the press in theater was a good public relations gimmick for the military as well. The presence of the media in theater recording the performance of the troops allowed the military to display a positive professional image.

The scope of the embedding was vast. Nearly 400 journalists were embedded in the Army, 18 in the Air Force, about 150 in the Marines, and 141 in the Navy.[59] About 100 of the total embedded press corps consisted of foreign reporters, including Al Jazeera reporters.[60] A range of press agencies were involved, including prime-time

---

[57] Quoted in Dilanian, Ken, "Seeking the Inside Story in an Iraq War," *Philadelphia Inquirer,* March 16, 2003.

[58] Quoted in Kurtz, Howard, "Media Notes: A Battle Plan for the '03 Campaign," *Washington Post,* January 20, 2003.

[59] Cooper and Cloud, "Branches of U.S. Military Fight over Media Attention in Iraq."

[60] Interviews revealed that Al Jazeera's embedded reporters were attached to "rear area" units, which were assigned to (and never left) Kuwait.

news networks (e.g., ABC, CBS, NBC, and CNN), daily newspapers (e.g., *The New York Times* and *Washington Post*), popular magazines (e.g., *Rolling Stone* and *People*), and cable channels (e.g., MTV). The British troops also allowed journalists to be embedded into their own units. According to the British Ministry of Defense, there were about 128 embedded journalists from British media.[61] The total number of reporters deployed during the major combat phase of this operation was larger than anything seen before, with approximately 1,445 reporters obtaining credentials as "unilaterals."[62] All tolled, approximately 2,200 reporters were in theater.

Although the embedded press system was intended partly to benefit U.S. military operations, the DoD did not control all aspects of the coverage, and sometimes "unexpected reporting" occurred as a result. For example, at one point the Pentagon was outpaced by the press, leaving Secretary of Defense Donald Rumsfeld to face Al Jazeera footage of American prisoners of war and casualties during his interview on CBS' *Face the Nation.* Also worthy of note is the negative reporting during the second week of the war—which were considered by some as "week-two jitters." Newspaper headlines are indicative of the negative, pessimistic coverage for that week, even though from a military standpoint the operation was proceeding very smoothly and would successfully conclude shortly thereafter.[63]

---

[61] Hoon, Geoff, "No Lens Is Wide Enough to Show the Big Picture: We Are Winning, But You Wouldn't Know It from Some of the Television Reports," *London Times*, March 28, 2003.

[62] Leiby, Richard, "'Unilaterals,' Crossing the Lines: Reporters Who Venture out on Their Own Can Find the Going Deadly," *Washington Post*, March 23, 2003.

[63] For example, headlines included: "Questions Raised About Invasion Force: Some Ex-Gulf War Commanders Say U.S. Needs More Troops, Another Armored Division," (Loeb, Vernon, and Thomas E. Ricks, *Washington Post*, March 25, 2003); "Allies' Pre-War Assumptions Fall Short As Iraqi Resistance Stiffens" (Slavin, Barbara, and Vivienne Walt, *USA Today*, March 25, 2003); "Sandstorm Brings Forces to Grinding Halt" (Knickmeyer, Ellen, *Washington Times*, March 25, 2003); "Iraq Forcing Longer, Conventional War" (Brownstein, Ronald, *Los Angeles Times*, March 26, 2003); "Former Commanders Question U.S. Strategy" (Cooper, Richard T., and Paul Richter, *Los Angeles Times*, March 26, 2003); and "War Could Last Months, Officers Say" (Ricks, Thomas E., *Washington Post*, March 27, 2003).

> From the mobile command vantage point, the war was going exceedingly well—even during the weekend of March 29, when Army generals, TV generals, and the press worried that a quagmire had swallowed the U.S. forces. The Marines were gaining excellent yardage on Baghdad—which conflicted with the TV images of selected units.[64]

Many in the military were unhappy about the disconnect between military progress and the image of stagnation and failure shown in the media.

A few reporters also violated the ground rules and engaged in "irresponsible" reporting, as had been feared during the planning phase of embedding—though one of the most famous cases involved a reporter who was not embedded, but acting as a "unilateral" journalist and co-locating with troops. Philip Smucker of *The Christian Science Monitor* revealed the exact location of a unit he was traveling with during a live interview with CNN.[65] Reporting for Fox News, Geraldo Rivera, who was not "embedded" but was assigned to the 101st Airborne Division, drew a map in the sand during a broadcast that contained sufficient information to locate American troops. However, such instances were rare. Fewer than half a dozen reporters were disembedded for improper reporting of events.

And despite such problems, on the whole, embedding allowed the military to meet its goals for news coverage during the major combat operations phase of OIF. The military benefited, for example, from having independent and credible reporters on hand to verify or debunk claims about what was really occurring on the battlefield. For instance, the Iraqi Minister of Information used embedded press coverage of the skirmish in Umm Qasr to illustrate his (false) claim that U.S. forces were bogged down by Iraqi resistance. Rejecting this claim, *USA Today* published a report by an embedded journalist the following day showing that the Marines were moving through Umm

---

[64] Shafer, Jack, "Embeds and Unilaterals," *Slate,* May 1, 2003. Online at http://slate.msn.com/id/2082412 (as of June 25, 2003).

[65] Kurtz, Howard, "Unembedded Journalist's Report Provokes Military Ire," *Washington Post,* March 27, 2003.

Qasr very slowly in order to make sure no civilians were mixed in with the Iraqi soldiers. Embedded reporters also confirmed the wide use of precision bombs in this war, thus mitigating some initial reports equating the bombing to the "carpet bombing" of London in World War II. Moreover, when incorrect reports did go out, the press typically issued follow-up reports or corrections, which worked to instill credibility in the Pentagon's claims and its mission.

The press also benefited from opportunities to pool their efforts and share stories in theater. Newspaper coverage of the major combat operations phase of OIF typically drew on the work of multiple reporters—even a single newspaper article might be the result of collaboration among different embedded journalists and reporters at U.S. Central Command briefings. While some voiced concerns that embedding might result in a "soda-straw-view" effect (i.e., the idea that a single embedded reporter would have a limited view of the war, akin to seeing the world through a soda straw), the press, especially print media, worked to avoid such problems. Stories often combined reports from many sources (multiple embedded journalists, official briefings, other news outlets) to assemble better "big picture" views.

## Observations

This chapter has traced the back-and-forth interactions between the press and the media over the past several decades. In Vietnam, the press enjoyed high levels of access to events, largely because of the relatively amicable relationship that had developed between the press and the military, particularly in World War II. However, this relationship experienced a significant shift during the Vietnam War—news coverage critical of both the war and the military engendered tensions. The legacy of these tensions significantly influenced military-press relations in later operations in Grenada, Panama, and the first Gulf War. Another notable shift occurred during the first Gulf War, however, establishing the basis for new kinds of press access, which ultimately led to the embedded press system used at the onset of Operation Iraqi Freedom.

Table 3.1 summarizes the historical conflicts discussed, the major issues regarding news coverage of that conflict, and the legacies influencing future press-military relations.

As illustrated in this chapter, the relationship between the military and the press included both episodes of conflict and opportunities for cooperation. While the legacy of Vietnam continued to reso-

**Table 3.1**
**Summary of Cases, News Coverage Issues, and Legacies**

| Conflict | Issue Regarding News Coverage | Legacy |
|---|---|---|
| Vietnam | Press feels military has betrayed its trust; military is unhappy with coverage | Long-standing mutual mistrust |
| Grenada | Military focuses on need for operational security; press is denied access | Press pools |
| Panama | Press pool is not properly implemented because of logistical problems | Further reform |
| First Gulf War | Press is given limited access, censorship, "spoon feeding"; military takes a more proactive role in seeking to use news coverage for its own benefit | Legal pressure |
| Somalia | Press gains access before military humanitarian operation begins; military is unhappy with some of the resulting coverage | The press "turns the tables" |
| Haiti | Press again gains access before operation begins, but coverage is more satisfactory to military | Cooperation |
| Bosnia | First use of embedded press system, though on a small scale | Precedent set for expanded use of embedded press |
| Kosovo | Press cannot easily cover air war; enemy central command provides its own information to media | Importance of independent press versus enemy propaganda |
| Afghanistan | Difficulty in covering special operations; press complains about restrictions on access | Pressure to allow some access to operations regardless of type |
| Major combat operations of OIF | Embedded press versus unilaterals; other topics documented later in this book | Expectation of embedded press for future operations |

nate for years afterward (and in some ways remains an issue today), the history of military-press relations since Vietnam also shows a gradual awareness on the part of both institutions of common ground. Each institution realized, further, that its own goals for wartime news coverage (e.g., press access and good military public relations) were in many instances compatible, if not identical, with the goals of the other institution.

The changes in military press-relations occurred in response to pressures from within both institutions—as well as to other factors. For example, greater restrictions on press access after Vietnam were in part due to attitudes of the military leadership, which was mainly composed of those who had been junior officers in Vietnam. However, the resulting press policies also responded to pressure from reporters, who were increasingly skeptical of the military and of authority in general following Vietnam and the Watergate scandal. Changes in access arrangements after Grenada, Panama, and the first Gulf War were partly the result of pressure from the media—and media willingness to file lawsuits and to mobilize its interests. At the same time, technological developments also played a role in facilitating, even forcing, change. Moreover, changes within the military's leadership structure and a growing recognition of the positive benefits of news coverage motivated the military to become more media savvy and to change its policy regarding press access.

Military-press relations have also evolved in response to the specific individuals and personalities who have been involved in the decisionmaking process. The importance of individual commitments cannot be underestimated. For example, the success of the embedded press system in Iraq depends not just on the designs of its architects at the DoD and in the press corps but also on the commitment of the unit commanders responsible for implementing it:

> The embed program proved to be only as good as the commanders overseeing it. Embeds on the carrier USS *Abraham Lincoln* had to mutiny against the military to report the war. When they boarded the ship, Rear Adm. John M. Kelly forced them to agree to ground rules that were more restrictive than the Pentagon-imposed rules. The Washington Post's Lyndsey Layton,

> who covered the Navy's air war from the carrier, says the rear admiral assigned a Navy "minder" to sit in on every interview and note every question asked and every reply made. He banned reporters from the general mess deck, essentially preventing them from interacting with sailors. After five days of this treatment, Layton and her colleagues took their complaint to Navy brass in Bahrain. Only then were the ad hoc restrictions on reporters' movements lifted; eventually the escorts, who had previously shadowed the reporters' every step, vanished.[66]

While this passage illustrates the role played by unit commanders, it also highlights the important roles played by individuals higher up the military chain of command and by the individual reporters themselves. Layton herself was instrumental in making the complaint, but she was successful in changing the press policy (or in ensuring that the decided-upon policy would be enforced) only because she found a sympathetic audience and a sufficient level of commitment at a higher level of military command. Indeed, the success of the embedded press approach depended on personal commitment from the highest levels of the DoD, particularly Secretary Rumsfeld, who wanted press in Iraq and wanted the military to faithfully execute his plans for press-military relations. As Galloway notes regarding the regulations concerning embedded press:

> These rules carry the return address of Secretary of Defense Don Rumsfeld. They state very plainly that no local commander shall seize press materials or prevent their transmission. He has authority only to restrict press transmissions during an ongoing operation if such transmission may compromise security. Of course there will be flareups here and there. But the SecDef's intent is very plain and clear, and woe betide the lt. col. or col. who violates those rules.[67]

---

[66] Shafer, "Embeds and Unilaterals."

[67] Galloway, Joe, "Sign 'Rules for Media' or Not?" *KnightRidder,* February 20, 2003. Online at http://www.realcities.com/mld/krwashington/news/special_packages/galloway/5226190.html (as of September 23, 2003).

High-level commitment to whatever press policies are in place will continue to be necessary for their successful implementation, particularly as long as the legacy of Vietnam continues to hold sway over some individual military officers and until comfortable relations with the press become the norm rather than the exception.

While this chapter has focused on how the embedded press came to be, the next chapter will compare the embedded press system of access with other possible approaches and will lay out a method for measuring the success of the embedded press and other methods.

CHAPTER FOUR

# Systems for Press Access and Measures for Evaluating Outcomes

> Engaging the press while engaging the enemy is taking on one adversary too many.
>
> — Lieutenant Colonel James Kevin Lovejoy[1]

Having considered the relationship between the press and the military in the abstract and then examined the history of press-military relations, we now describe our approach for evaluating the embedded press system in relation to other ways of organizing press-military relations.

There are two parts to this chapter. First, we describe the four idealized systems for organizing military-press relations that will be evaluated in this book. In this discussion, we emphasize the access strategies at the core of each system: denial of access, press pools, unilateral journalism, and embedded press. We emphasize access because of the criticality of this goal from the press's perspective. Access is a key press goal for news coverage and one that facilitates other goals (providing news to the public and maintaining the quality of coverage). We discuss the access strategies in relation to a series of strategies for protecting operational security. Operational security is critical to the military's main mission and to its goals with regard to news coverage. The access strategies and operational security strategies

[1] Lovejoy, James Kevin, "Improving Media Relations," *Military Review,* Vol. 82, No. 1, January/February 2002.

can be combined to produce a system for managing military-press relations.

The second part of the chapter lays out the dimensions of our evaluation of the embedded press and other systems for organizing press-military relations. In that section we briefly describe the measures used in our analysis. These measures are based on the goals for news coverage that were described in Chapter Two.

## Systems for Organizing Military-Press Relations

In this section we will discuss a variety of access strategies and operational security strategies that may be used as part of a system for organizing military-press relations.

### Access Strategies for Organizing Press-Military Relations

> After more than 130 years, the fundamental dispute between the American media and the American military has changed hardly at all. The essential argument is still about access. How much should the press be allowed to know and see of the conduct of battle?[2]

As suggested by the case studies discussed in the previous chapter, a range of access strategies have been used to guide military-press relations during wartime. Across access strategies, three key factors vary:

- *The number of reporters to be provided access.* For example, during the Iraq war, the target number of embedded reporters was 500, though that number ultimately rose to between 600 and 700.
- *The sources of information made available to reporters.* Potential sources include centralized military-provided information, direct contact with soldiers, eyewitness accounts of combat, contact with enemy combatants, and contact with civilians in the combat zone. "Unfettered access" to any and all sources is the jour-

[2] Andrews, "The Media and the Military," p. 78.

nalistic touchstone, in that this is the default for press access outside the combat environment.

- *The level of safety provided to reporters in the field.* Plans for reporter safety, including acceptable levels of risk, decisions about who should accept the burden of risk, and responsibilities for ensuring safety, are important considerations in an access strategy.

While any number of access strategies are possible, for purposes of our evaluation, four types of access strategies will be used to illustrate some key distinctions in the level of access provided. The idealized types discussed here range along a continuum from most restrictive to least restrictive. All of these strategies have historical precedent, although in the overall scheme of military-press relations, variations on these strategies, along with hybrid forms, have also been used.

**Denial of Access.** At one end of the continuum is denial of access. Although this arrangement is never popular with the press, the military's focus on operational security often means that a journalist's request for access is denied. The military can opt for—and implement—complete denial of access in situations where interdiction of the entire battle space is possible and relatively easy. This was the case at the start of the conflicts in Grenada, Panama, and the first Gulf War. In other situations, the military cannot control access to such a high degree, as was seen, for example, in Somalia and Haiti where the press gained access before the military began its operations.

Part of the reason denial of access is so unpopular among journalists is that it doesn't necessarily reduce the amount of *coverage* of the war (i.e., the amount of airtime or printed pages devoted to the issue), but alters the scope and quality of that coverage by limiting reporters to official sources only.

> The new system is right out of a Madison Avenue manual for publicity blitz. If you want pictures, you will get more that you can possibly use, but they will be our pictures. If you want quotes, you will get them by the hour, but they will be our

> quotes. If you want access, you will be personally escorted to the front, but we will determine where and when you get there.[3]

While denial of access as an entire and exclusive system is less likely today given the historical antecedents, denial of access on a smaller scale is still possible. On the battlefield, the military tends to hold all the cards. Even when a journalist has, in principle, been given access (e.g., as an embed), that journalist can still be denied access to a specific story by an individual soldier or unit commander.

While the press is broadly opposed to being denied access, there are situations in which journalists accept, or show greater understanding of, the need for access to be denied. For example, journalists have generally accepted that special operations should remain a bastion of secrecy.

**Press Pools.** A limited form of access is made possible in a press pool, in which a small number of preselected reporters are allowed access to some otherwise unavailable source of information. However, in exchange for that access, all journalists must pool their reporting with that of other news agencies, so that no exclusives or scoops can be claimed by pool participants.

According to Combelles-Siegel, the press pool system as used to date addresses three specific military concerns about access: (1) to make it possible to activate a small group of journalists while maintaining operational security, (2) to make sure that the pool is transported to an event, and (3) to make sure that communication facilities are available to file stories in a timely manner.[4] But, as Combelles-Siegel points out, the creation of a press pool doesn't necessarily guarantee access to information sources. Reporters can be members of the official pool without necessarily having access to newsworthy sources.

Press pools can be useful in several situations. First, in a situation that calls for operational surprise, a press pool provides a means

---

[3] Andrews, "The Media and the Military," p. 83.

[4] Combelles-Siegel, *The Troubled Path to the Pentagon's Rules on Media Access to the Battlefield, Grenada to Today*, p. 16.

of allowing some limited coverage of what is otherwise a secret operation. Second, the pool might be useful in situations in which only a limited number of reporters can be accommodated. Third, in some situations, networks might want to leave only a few cameras and reporters in place and then share the feed with everyone as a "pooled" resource. The latter situation, though technically a pool, isn't implemented by the military and is less of a system than a shared convenience.

**Embedded Press.** As indicated by our discussion of the embedded press in the previous chapter, embedding gives journalists direct access to troops and to any combat those troops see. "Embedding means living, eating, moving in combat with the unit that you're attached to."[5] "Embedded press," at its simplest, suggests reporters traveling with military units, seeing what they see. There are many ways to imagine the logistical details of this system. We have only the single largest use of embedding, the major combat operations phase of Operation Iraqi Freedom, for an example. The system as implemented for Iraq was "embed for life," meaning that reporters would not move around among units; further, a reporter who leaves his or her embedding unit may not be able to return. While an embedded press system provides access, the military retains a large measure of control over that access, determining, for example, which journalists receive the most desirable embedding assignments.

**Unilaterals.** At the opposite end of the continuum from "denial of access" is "unilateral" journalism, under which reporters operate with broad freedom of access. Unilateral journalism is as closely akin as possible to the "standard" day-to-day model of news reporting and collecting. Unilateral journalism has historically taken two forms: freedom to travel with troops (but without the sort of official assignments used with the embedded press) and "cowboy" or "four-wheel-drive" journalism, in which journalists do not travel with specific troops, but travel on their own, and at their own risk.

---

[5] Bryan Whitman quoted in Ricchiardi, "Preparing for War."

Unilateral journalism can be short on safety. Further, the need for military resources to rescue supposedly independent unilateral journalists is a very real possibility, as discussed by John Donvan, who was a unilateral in Iraq, in a recent panel discussion:

> We also had nonstop dialogues in the car, should we go down this road, is it safe, is it not safe? But one of the dialogues we had constantly in the car was, what are we going to do if we get into trouble? We came here, we're working outside the system that the Pentagon offered. What if we get into trouble? Do we have the right to call for help, which is what the *Newsweek* guy did? We ultimately concluded that we didn't. If we chose to come in this way, we didn't have the right to ask for help. As one of us said, how are you going to tell some Marine's mother that he died trying to extract some idiot journalist who got himself into trouble?[6]

### Operational Security Strategies

Access to news sources is critical for journalists if they are to fulfill their reporting mission. For the military, a key goal with regard to news coverage is to ensure that reporters do not compromise the operational security of the military mission, thereby jeopardizing the success of the operation. Thus, systems of press-military relations typically contain some form of strategy for maintaining operational security. There are a number of different strategies for protecting operational security that can be attached to any of the broader access strategies with greater or lesser success. We focus on three of these: credentialing, censorship, and "security at the source."

**Credentialing.** One approach to maintaining operational security is for the military to take reporters into their confidence and then ask that, on their professional honor, they not violate that confidence. This is somewhat risky, however, given the goals of news reporting and the wide variety of interpretations of journalistic ethics among reporters. A less risky strategy is to exact a commitment from report-

[6] Council on Foreign Relations, *Embedded Journalists in Iraq.*

ers not to reveal certain kinds of information before taking them into confidence (or allowing them special access, or whatever is being considered). Should a reporter violate the terms of these credentials, the reporter can be ejected from the theater and prosecuted or otherwise censured. Clear guidelines, coupled with professional integrity and the threat of censure, have proven to be a surprisingly resilient method of protecting operations.

When treated as professionals and offered military confidences, reporters have historically proven worthy of that confidence. In return, the "military leadership is willing to take news organizations into their confidence in some pre-operational situations, as they did prior to the aborted Haiti invasion."[7] While actual terms of credentials differ, the agreement established for embedded reporters in Iraq precluded their reporting on anything that would endanger operational security, specifically troop strengths, locations, and strategies.[8] Likewise, the military reserved the right to notify next of kin before casualties are identified by name in the news.

**Censorship.** The other traditional means of protecting operational security without denying access is censorship. In a modern American value system, "censorship" is typically a bad word. However, in a world where the identification of threats to operational security requires a judgment call, censorship (or "security review" as it is referred to in military parlance) is the only way to take that judgment out of the hands of the reporter and put it back into the hands of the military.

> Many news executives and reporters see no difficulty with a limited degree of censorship in extraordinary circumstances, even in the field, as long as the guidelines are developed in advance and are understood and strictly obeyed by both sides.[9]

---

[7] Aukofer and Lawrence, *America's Team*, p. 4.

[8] Shafer, "Embeds and Unilaterals."

[9] Aukofer and Lawrence, *America's Team*, p. 3.

In fact, Moskos argues that the presence of censorship during World War II meant that there was more candor and openness between the press and military officials than there has been since that time, simply because everything that the reporter wrote would be reviewed for security purposes.[10]

However, regardless of possible benefits of security review or some willingness on the part of news agencies to accept some restriction on what can be reported, outright censorship is a thing of the past.[11] This is largely because of two factors: first, the expectation of live news, and second, the incredible technological advances that allow live news broadcasts from almost anywhere, making censorship nigh-impossible.

**"Security at the Source."** The military's current means for reconciling the impossibility of censorship and the imperatives of access is a strategy known as "security at the source." This strategy requires soldiers and officers to be circumspect about what they say to reporters. Soldiers are advised to answer questions only about things of which they have direct knowledge or that they do or have done. They are discouraged from speculating about high-level strategy or spreading rumors. One of our reporter informants overheard an instruction that summarized this strategy best: "only speak to your pay grade." This is noticeably different from "don't talk to reporters" and is presented in standard public affairs instructions as being responsible with, and accountable for, what is presented to the press.

### Summary of Systems for Organizing Military-Press Relations

Table 4.1 summarizes some of the properties of the four idealized access strategies and the two security strategies discussed above. Each access strategy is given a notional value concerning: (1) what the reporter can witness, (2) the level of access (unit access, field/theater access, and access to observe combat), (3) the depth and breadth of

---

[10] Moskos, *The Media and the Military in Peace and Humanitarian Operations*.

[11] Aukofer and Lawrence, *America's Team*, p. 3.

**Table 4.1**
**Notional Relative Design Properties of Access and Security Strategies**

| | | Access Strategy | | | | Security Strategy | |
|---|---|---|---|---|---|---|---|
| | Considerations | Denial of Access | Press Pool | Embedded Press | Unilateral Journalism | *Credentials* | *Security Review* |
| | What the reporter sees | Nothing | What the military wants | What the unit sees | Whatever you dare | +/– | |
| Access | Controls on unit access | High | Medium/high | Low | High | – | |
| | Controls on field access | High | High | Low/medium | Low | | |
| | Combat access | Low | Low | High | Whatever you dare | | |
| Coverage | Depth of coverage | Low | Low/medium | High | Medium | | – |
| | Breadth of coverage | Low | Medium | Low | Medium | | – |
| | Threat to operational security | Low | Low/medium | High/medium | Low/medium | + | + |
| | Institutional constraints (reporting delays) | High | Medium | Low | Low | | – |

NOTE: +/– is mixed, – is negative, and + is positive/favorable.
RAND *MG200-4.1*

coverage, and (4) the potential threats to operational security as well as potential constraints on reporting.

This table illustrates some of the considerations and tradeoffs that designers of a system of wartime press-military relations might take into consideration. Several access and security strategies can be combined to help the press and the military meet their respective goals. Looking at the column for the embedded press system, we see that, in relation to other types of systems, the embedded press is superior in terms of perspective, access, and depth of coverage. As the table indicates, in an environment where the threat to operational security posed by having reporters in combat can be mitigated by credentials, professionalism, and earned trust—and coupled with an access strategy that encourages broader coverage—the embedded press system is very attractive by design.

### Implementation of Systems for Managing Press-Military Relations

Given these "idealized types" of access and security strategies, how do these systems for managing press-military relations translate into reality? In Table 4.2, we present a holistic view of the access and security strategies employed in six selected military operations. Table 4.2 estimates the number of reporters in theater and attempts to indicate whether or not specific access and security strategies were employed during the operation.

Table 4.2 provides a quick summary of some of the characteristics of the systems of press relations actually used in some of the historical cases discussed in Chapter Three. Of particular note is the fact that none of the "idealized" systems of press relations ever appears in a pure form. While every operation has an identifiable core system of press-military relations, that core system is always accompanied by, or followed by,[12] other systems.

---

[12] Consider the table entry for Grenada. The press was excluded for the first 48 hours of the Grenada operation, which included the entire combat phase of the operation. This exclusion was followed by several days of limited press pools and finally gave way to unfettered unilateral coverage.

**Table 4.2**
**Major Access and Security Strategies During Significant Combat Phase of Selected Operations**

| | Operations | | | | | |
|---|---|---|---|---|---|---|
| Variables | Grenada | Panama | 1st Gulf War | Somalia | Bosnia | Iraq |
| Estimated number of reporters | 600 | 800 | 1,600 (186 in pools) | 600 | 33 embeds in 15 units | 2,200 (over 600 embeds) |
| Access strategy | | | | | | |
| Access denial | Y | Y | Y/N | N | N | N |
| Press pools | Y | Y | Y | Y | N | N |
| Embedded press | N | N | N | N | Y | Y |
| Unilateral journalism | N | Y | Y | Y | Y | Y |
| Security strategy | | | | | | |
| Credentials | Y | Y | Y | Y | Y | Y |
| Security reviews | N | N | Y | N | N | N |

RAND *MG200-4.2*

## Measures for Evaluating the Embedded Press System

Having examined different ideal systems for organizing press-military relations, we now consider how the performance of those systems might be evaluated. In constructing the relevant dimensions of evaluation, we have chosen to focus on discernable outcomes based on the goals for news coverage we derived from existing scholarship (see Chapter Two).

We have identified relevant measures for evaluating each of these goals. Table 4.3 lists the goals/outcomes and proposed ways to measure those outcomes. For further discussion of the development and details of these measures, please see Appendix B.

**Table 4.3**
**Outcomes and Measures for Press-Military Relations**

| Goals for News Coverage | Measures |
|---|---|
| **Military** | |
| Do not allow news coverage to compromise operational security | Numbers of actions postponed or cancelled due to operational security concerns<br>Number of press credentials revoked or reporters chastised for security violations<br>Case analysis of potential operational security violations |
| Fulfill legal obligations regarding press access | |
| Press given sufficient access | Access-related lawsuits<br>News analysis of press complaints about access |
| Public informed | Public opinion data: satisfied with coverage; percentage following issue |
| Use news coverage to support military mission | |
| Obtain good public relations | |
| Public | Public opinion data<br>Surveys |
| Press | Surveys<br>News analysis |
| International audience | Public opinion data<br>Surveys |
| Build credibility | Public opinion data<br>Surveys<br>NCI |
| Support information operations | News analysis for counter-propaganda<br>Case analysis |

**Table 4.3—continued**

| | |
|---|---|
| **Press** | |
| Gain access to newsworthy information | |
| Satisfactory access arrangement | Surveys of reporters<br>Content analysis of sources of information<br>Tabulation of access opportunities offered<br>Case analysis |
| Safety of reporters | Number of reporters killed or injured |
| Provide newsworthy information to the public | |
| Fulfill 4th Estate obligations | Public opinion data<br>Surveys |
| Build market share | |
| Print | Circulation |
| Television | Ratings |
| Maintain quality of news | |
| Fairness, objectivity, and accuracy | Content analysis; identification of erroneous stories<br>Awards |
| Credibility | Public opinion data<br>Surveys<br>Content analysis: retractions/corrections<br>Case analysis |
| **Public** | |
| Gain information | |
| Satisfied with coverage | Public opinion data |
| Informed by coverage | Polls and surveys |
| Be "well-served" | Not easily measured |

NOTE: NCI is National Credibility Index. See Appendix B for further details.

Since the analysis here relies primarily on historical case studies and holistic impressions of the outcomes for a given case, we focus the measures offered in Table 4.3 on quantitative evaluations for future research, where possible. The measures proposed are of three types: measurement through poll or survey, measurement through counts (content analysis or simple tabulation of events of certain kinds), and measurement through "case analysis" or other qualitative or narrative assessment.

Note that, for many of these goals, the best way to measure them is through case analysis or other qualitative means. While we support the use of several quantitative measures in the evaluation of the embedded press, the comparative historical work we have done here remains a valuable contribution, and the methods we use here should continue to be used in research in this area to capture the dynamics of the relationship between the military and the press. Again, a more detailed discussion of the various methods we propose for collecting data for these measures can be found in Appendix B.

Now that we have defined a range of systems for organizing military-press relations and have identified the measures used in our analysis, we are ready to present the results of our evaluation.

CHAPTER FIVE

# Preliminary Evaluations of the Embedded Press and Other Systems for Organizing Press-Military Relations

> We've never had a war like this. . . . We got inundated by close-ups. Somebody's got to take a step back and give a little perspective.
>
> — Tom Bettag[1]

We move now to our evaluation of the embedded press system. This chapter presents a comparative/historical analysis of the embedded press system relative to other access strategies for press-military relations (denial of access, press pools, and unilateral journalism), with consideration given to the modifying presence of such security strategies as credentialing and security review. We consider these strategies both in the actual historical circumstances in which they have been employed and in abstract, generic contexts. Where data are available, we have supplemented this narrative-based analysis with quantitative findings based on the outcomes and measures listed in the previous chapter.

---

[1] Project for Excellence in Journalism, *Embedded Reporters: What Are Americans Getting?* Washington, D.C., 2003. Online at http://www.journalism.org/resources/research/reports/war/embed/default.asp (as of September 23, 2003).

## The Embedded Press System

This section notionally scores or evaluates the embedded press system as used in Iraq on each of the goals/outcomes discussed in Chapter Four. Where statistical data are lacking, we resort to outcome evaluation notionally based on the historical narrative.

### Military Goals and Measures

**Do Not Allow News Coverage to Compromise Operational Security.** Considered in the abstract, embedded press is one of the most vulnerable systems of press-military relations from an operational security standpoint. Reporters witness action firsthand and are often privy to operational plans; further, in the contemporary era, they have the technology available to transmit that information immediately and live. This threat is mitigated only by commitments made in credentialing agreements and by the journalistic and personal integrity of the reporters, and this mitigation is bolstered by the additional understanding and sympathy a reporter gains by spending an extended period of time with a single group of soldiers.

Given the potential magnitude of the threat, we find that operational security in Iraq was generally intact and protected far more than it was violated; however, it was also the case that operational security was not perfect and was not close to the military's target threshold—"secure." We were unable to gain access to data regarding the number of operations postponed or cancelled because of news coverage, but these data may become available at a later point. We are aware of less than a half-dozen disembeddings for violations of operational security. We are unaware of any *compromises* of operational security, where Iraqi forces took advantage of news violations of operational security.[2] Our minimally informed estimate based on accounts and reports we have collected is that violations of operational security had no consequences for overall operational success. It is our estimation, however, that operational security remains the greatest

[2] We have not looked in the classified realm at all, so it is possible that such violations did take place and are simply not discussed in open source material.

vulnerability of an embedded press system, and future planners of press-military relations should continue to consider innovative approaches to increasing security with media coverage.

**Fulfill Legal Obligations Regarding Press Access.** Embedded press as implemented in Iraq shines in terms of fulfilling legal obligations. Although the use of the embedded press may in theory have increased risks to operational security, the approach allowed for broad press access to troops and fighting, making great quantities of information available to the public.

Figure 5.1 shows the number of articles that were published on countries of interest over time. For the given period of time, Eric Larson used the Lexis-Nexis Academic Universe search option to see how many articles in *The New York Times* mentioned specific words—e.g., "Iraq" or "Somalia"—and he recorded the number of articles on the topic in that span of time.[3] *The New York Times* was chosen because it is considered a reasonable benchmark that is representative of journalistic coverage on a given issue. Since we are largely interested in *change* in the level of coverage over time, any source-specific bias from *The New York Times* would not affect our variable of interest. First, as the figure shows, the number of articles published on these countries is greater during periods of major military operations than during other periods. What this suggests is that the level of coverage a given issue receives depends on whether there is or is not a major U.S. military operation. Second, the level of coverage differed depending on whether the military operation was large or small in scale and size. As the data show, the number of articles published on Iraq was greatest during the major combat operations phase of Operation Iraqi Freedom. While this may in part be the result of the presence of the new embedded press system, there are other factors—such as technology, the number of reporters, the type of military engagement, etc.—that may have influenced these outcomes. Regardless, coverage of the major combat phase of OIF far outstripped coverage of any other recent conflict.

---

[3] We thank Eric Larson for compiling these data.

**Figure 5.1**
**Volume of News Coverage of Selected Countries over Time**

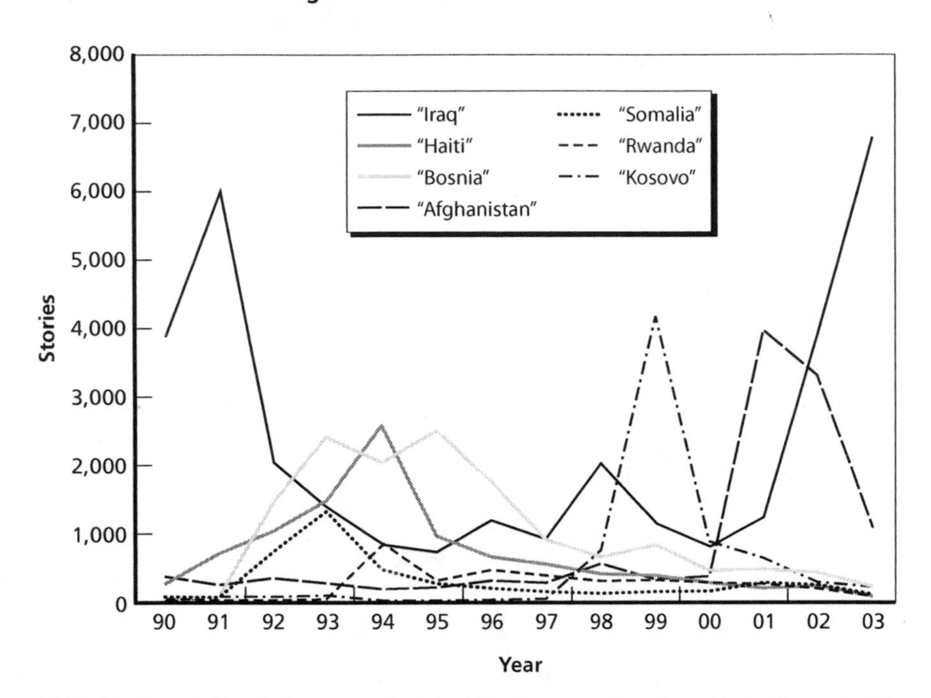


SOURCE: Unpublished data compiled by Eric Larson using New York Times Article Archive, 1990–2003, *The New York Times on the Web*, http://www.nytimes.com.
RAND *MG200-5.1*

**Use News Coverage to Support the Military Mission.** *Obtain good public relations.* Embedded press during major combat operations in Iraq, coupled with the decisive military victory and the by-and-large exemplary performance of U.S. forces, resulted in excellent public relations for the military. Public support for the military remained high, even during the second week of the war (discussed as "week-two jitters" in Chapter Three) when several negative stories appeared. While direct support for the military wasn't polled regularly, Table 5.1 shows poll results regarding support for the decision to go to war in Iraq, which also could have been affected by the week-

**Table 5.1 Support for Decision to Go to War in Iraq[a] (in percentage)**

| | Date | | | |
|---|---|---|---|---|
| **Response** | **3/20/03** | **3/23/03** | **3/27/03** | **4/3/03** |
| Strongly support | 53 | 55 | 58 | 58 |
| Somewhat support | 19 | 17 | 16 | 15 |
| Somewhat oppose | 8 | 10 | 8 | 8 |
| Strongly oppose | 18 | 16 | 16 | 16 |
| No opinion | 2 | 2 | 3 | 4 |

SOURCES: ABC News/*The Washington Post* poll conducted March 20, 2003, n = 506, Roper Center at University of Connecticut, *Public Opinion Online*, accessed through Lexis-Nexis (as of July 27, 2004); *The Washington Post* poll conducted March 23, 2003, n = 580, Roper Center at University of Connecticut, *Public Opinion Online*, accessed through Lexis-Nexis (as of July 27, 2004); ABC News/*The Washington Post* poll conducted March 27, 2003, n = 508, Roper Center at University of Connecticut, *Public Opinion Online*, accessed through Lexis-Nexis (as of July 27, 2004); and ABC News/*The Washington Post* poll conducted April 3, 2003, n = 511, Roper Center at University of Connecticut, *Public Opinion Online*, accessed through Lexis-Nexis (as of July 27, 2004).

NOTE: Percentages are rounded.

[a] Poll question: Do you support or oppose the United States having gone to war with Iraq?

two jitters. Table 5.1 includes a poll at the outset of the war and one for each week of major combat operations. Support begins high and remains high over the course of operations.

The use of the embedded press system also seems to have had a positive influence on military relations with the press. Overall, there were far fewer press complaints during this war than seen in previous major conventional operations, such as in Grenada, Panama, and the first Gulf War. Those complaints that did occur often focused on individual complaints from embedded reporters who "didn't see anything" (embedded with rear echelon units), but we saw no evidence that such views were widely shared across the broader press community. There were also complaints about the restrictions placed on unilateral reporters and the way they were treated as "second-class citizens" compared with the official embedded reporters. Finally, some members of the press complained about the lack of information and the credibility of information released by the U.S. Central Command.[4] It is unclear the extent to which these latter complaints were sincere or just part of somewhat institutionalized skepticism on the part of the press toward the military and the adversarial nature of the press.

Military public relations with international publics are much harder to disentangle from the popularity of U.S. policy abroad. The present analysis does not consider international public opinion, though we recognize it as an important outcome related to policies for press-military relations.

*Build credibility.* One poll conducted March 20–27, 2003, found that 40 percent of people surveyed had a "great deal" of confidence in military accuracy in reports about the Iraq war, with another 44 percent having a "fair amount" of confidence.[5]

In support of these data, our historical inquiry suggests that the military was very careful to protect its credibility and reasonably successful at doing so. While vague or tentative information released in U.S. Central Command briefings may have irked the press, the military took care to avoid making erroneous claims and carefully qualified the language of uncertainty when relaying unverified reports (of course, in several cases, this language of uncertainty was lost when relayed by the press; and, when reports subsequently proved false, the military still managed to get the heat for the error). As vexing as this is for the press, it seems to be the best strategy for the military and/or the government.

On the whole, demonstrated military commitment to the embedded press system, even in the face of events that did not show the military in a favorable light (such as the reporting of accidental civilian casualties at a checkpoint), served to increase and maintain mili-

[4] See, for example, Kampfer, John, "War Spin," *Correspondent*, BBC, first aired May 18, 2003. Online at http://news.bbc.co.uk/nol/shared/spl/hi/programmes/correspondent/transcripts/18.5.031.txt (as of September 17, 2003).

[5] The Pew Charitable Trusts, "TV Combat Fatigue on the Rise, but 'Embeds' Viewed Favorably," *Public Opinion and Polls,* Washington, D.C.: The Pew Research Center for the People & the Press, March 28, 2003. Online at http://www.pewtrusts.com/ideas/ideas_item.cfm?content_item_id=1522&content_type_id=18 (as of June 17, 2004).

tary credibility. (It should be noted that administration credibility and the failure to find Iraqi weapons of mass destruction remain a different issue.)

*Support successful information operations.* Operation Iraqi Freedom contained two examples of "honest" information operations, one more demonstrably successful than the other. The first was the "shock and awe" campaign at the beginning of the war. The media willingly showed the advancing might of U.S. armed forces, a display that, if it did not result in complete Iraqi submission, still likely had some intimidating effect. However, this effect would be very difficult to measure without data from former Iraqi soldiers, and the effect due to the "shock and awe" campaign would be very difficult to disentangle from that due to the preexisting reputation of the U.S. military.

The military was also able to use the press successfully to debunk false claims made by the Iraqi Minister of Information; independent media were able to "give the lie" to the Iraqi Minister of Information very effectively.

### Press Goals and Measures

**Gain Access to Newsworthy Information.** *Establish a satisfactory access arrangement.* Access is the highest priority of the "press" outcomes. As is clear from related military outcomes discussed above, the embedded press system as implemented allowed the press unprecedented access. However, "embedded press as implemented" includes not just the embedded press, but also other reporting and communications. As Laurence notes:

> It would not have been sufficient if it had been the *only* opportunity for press coverage in this war. But it's not. It's one element. The others balance it and broaden it and lead to the overall goal for both the military and the journalists, which is to provide an accurate picture of the war.[6]

---

[6] Laurence, John, "Embedding: A Military View," *Columbia Journalism Review,* web special, May/June 2003. Online at http://www.cjr.org/year/03/2/webspecial.asp (as of September 23, 2003).

The system of policies for press-military relations realized in Iraq should be considered "embedded press *plus*." While the showcase system of access was embedded press, it was supplemented by unilateral reporting and official information released by the U.S. Central Command. "Embedded press plus" afforded remarkable access in Iraq. Future planners of policies for press-military relations need to consider the type and the role of the "plus" access and coverage components.

*Ensure safety of reporters.* In general, risk to reporters under an embedded press system will be comparable to the risk to soldiers. The high level of access provided by an embedded press system is intertwined with a potentially increased level of risk. Embedded journalists bear approximately the same amount of risk as the soldiers they travel with. Risk to reporters serving as a unilateral component of "embedded press plus" may be considerably higher. Unilateral journalism in a combat environment remains very dangerous. Of the thirteen reporters killed during major combat operations in Iraq, only four were embedded journalists.

**Provide Newsworthy Information to the Public.** *Fulfill 4th Estate obligations.* As discussed earlier in this chapter, the public generally approved of the coverage of the war in Iraq. While public approval almost certainly results from a variety of factors, approval can reasonably be imputed to result at least in part from the information's effectiveness in helping people exercise their democratic rights. The press did a reasonably good job keeping the public informed and up to date on the progress of the war.

Figure 5.2 presents public opinion data regarding levels of press attention paid to certain topics. While public opinion data as a proxy for satisfaction of 4th Estate obligations are clearly conflated with other public preferences, these data can be considered indicative of satisfaction with many aspects of coverage, including all that a citizen would presumably want to know to exercise governmental oversight and participation in democracy. On all but three issues, the majority of respondents opined that the amount of news coverage given to a topic was "about right." Of the three issues where the majority

**Figure 5.2**
**Public Opinion of Attention Press Gave to Various Topics During War in Iraq[a]**

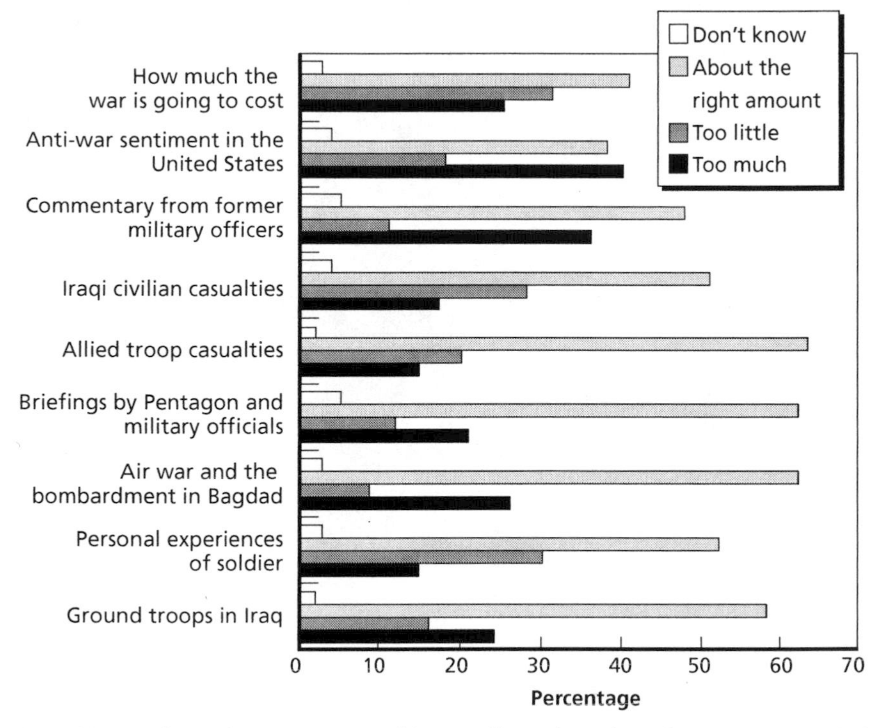


SOURCE: March/April 2003 "War Tracking" poll conducted April 2–7, 2003, n = 912, Roper Center at University of Connecticut, *Public Opinion Online*, accessed through Lexis-Nexis (as of July 27, 2004).

[a]Poll question: Now thinking specifically about the war in Iraq, please tell me if you think the press is giving too much, too little, or about the right amount of coverage to the following . . . .

**RAND** *MG200-5.2*

weren't satisfied, respondents varied over whether they thought the problem was "too little" or "too much" attention paid to that issue. On coverage given to "how much the war is going to cost," the split was fairly close. On coverage of anti-war sentiment, the vast majority of those who weren't satisfied with the level of coverage thought that there was too much coverage of this issue. This is unsurprising given the high levels of support for the war in general (see Table 5.1). The fact that 36 percent thought there was too much coverage of commentary from former military officers, especially given the high levels of support for the war, suggests this is an area in which the press might improve. Given that these different views about the amount of coverage did not seem to come at the expense of other important issues (the majority thought all other issues were given about the right amount of coverage), this imperfect measure suggests reasonably good 4th Estate performance.

*Build market share.* Did the embedded press system favor different press agencies or different media in the marketplace for news? While we did not seek data about the relative market success of different press agencies, we did find poll data asking respondents about their sources of information on the war in Iraq. Respondents were allowed to indicate receipt of information from multiple sources. Table 5.2 presents the results of this poll. We were unable to conduct a comparative analysis with similar data from another conflict, but our sense of the situation is that the embedded press system creates conditions favorable to live television coverage. It is unclear if this is at the expense of, or in addition to, other news formats.

**Table 5.2**
**Sources of Public Information About Iraq (in percentage)**

| News Source | Percentage |
|---|---|
| Cable news shows | 69 |
| Newspapers | 30 |
| Local news shows | 23 |
| Network news | 18 |
| Internet | 13 |
| Radio news | 8 |
| Family and friends | 4 |
| Other | 2 |

SOURCE: *Los Angeles Times* poll, April 2–7, 2003.

**Maintain Quality of News.** *Maintain fairness, objectivity, and accuracy.* Quality of journalism is particularly difficult to measure. The historical narrative reveals several concerns about journalistic quality during the war in Iraq, most having to do with fears of patriotic bias, or with embedded reporters losing their objectivity. The war was accompanied by a fair amount of journalistic "hand wringing" about the possibility of or the desirability of, "objectivity" or "neutrality." As one veteran war correspondent noted:

> When we didn't have a personal, a national stake in the war, we found it very easy to cover both sides of the story, and as I was saying before, to claim that we were neutral. I wasn't neutral in this war. I would try to be fair and honest, but I wanted the U.S. to prevail, once it got into it. I'm not neutral to that degree, and I can't claim neutrality on the battlefield out there.[7]

The Project for Excellence in Journalism (PEJ) has conducted a preliminary content analysis of several days of television coverage from the war in Iraq.[8]

> The embedded coverage, the research found, is largely anecdotal. It's both exciting and dull, combat focused, and mostly live and unedited. Much of it lacks context but it is usually rich in detail. It has all the virtues and vices of reporting only what you can see.[9]

The PEJ's report concludes that coverage from the embedded press was of reasonably high quality, for what it was. While the PEJ's findings are preliminary and the results equivocal, we commend the approach.

Another approach to assessing quality in journalism is through public opinion data. Again, it is reasonable to assume some confounding of public perception of quality of journalism with aspects of

---

[7] Council on Foreign Relations, *Embedded Journalists in Iraq,* p. 12.

[8] Project for Excellence in Journalism, *Embedded Reporters.*

[9] Project for Excellence in Journalism, *Embedded Reporters,* p. 1.

content, but the measure is not wholly without merit. For example, we found one poll asking respondents to "rate the job news organizations . . . have done in covering . . . the war with Iraq" (Gallup, March 29–30, 2003).[10] This poll found that 38 percent considered it "excellent," 41 percent indicated "good," 13 percent "only fair," and 7 percent "poor."

Our view—based on public opinion data, the PEJ study, and the accounts and news analysis we encountered—is that coverage of major combat operations in Iraq was generally of "good" quality, but there is room for improvement. We address our specific concerns in the section on possible shortcomings of the embedded press system in the next chapter.

*Build credibility.* Credibility is particularly hard to nail down for the press because of its atomized nature; different press agencies deserve different levels of credibility; however, different people will mentally aggregate "press" at different levels; some might distinguish between print and television, while others might single out specific agencies for greater skepticism, and still others might consider the press as a single monolithic enterprise. Public opinion data don't help in this enterprise—surveys tend to ask only about "the press" or "the media," thus forcing respondents toward a monolithic response.

Clearly there were events during the war that could have taxed press credibility. Consider the number of factual errors recorded by Mitchell during the first week of the war:

> The war is only a week old and already the media has gotten at least 15 stories wrong or misreported a sliver of fact into a major event. Television news programs, of course, have been the prime culprits. Newspapers, while they have often gone along for the ride, have been much more nuanced and careful. Newspaper coverage has not been faultless, as photos and headlines often seem shock-and-awe-struck but, compared with TV, newspapers seem more editorially—and mentally—balanced. Some have

[10] Gallup, CNN, *USA Today* poll conducted March 29, 2003, n = 1,012, Roper Center at University of Connecticut, *Public Opinion Online*, accessed through Lexis-Nexis (as of July 27, 2004).

> actually displayed a degree of skepticism of claims made by the military and the White House—what used to be known as "journalism."[11]

These individual incidents aside, public opinion polls suggest that Iraq coverage improved the perception of the media among some members of the public, but worsened the perception of others. For example, a Princeton Survey Research Associates (PSRA)/ *Newsweek* poll (April 10–11, 2003) found that Iraq coverage made 46 percent of respondents think better of U.S. media and 30 percent worse.[12] Another poll (Fox News/Opinion Dynamics Poll, April 8–10, 2003) found that 61 percent of respondents believed that reporters were too eager to paint either a negative or a positive picture of the war.[13] This public view that the press is inclined to bias one way or the other is likely related to credibility and suggests a baseline expectation of bias that is not consonant with high credibility.

#### Public Goals and Measures

**Get Information.** Several of the public opinion polls already mentioned suggest that, by and large, the public was satisfied with the amount of wartime coverage. The data presented in Figure 5.1 suggest that there was sufficient volume of coverage for the public to be informed.

**Seek to Be "Well-Served."** Regarding the much "squishier" issue of whether or not the public was well-served, we have little that is concrete to discuss. If "well-served" is different from "satisfied," it might be possible to disentangle the two when an individual practice,

---

[11] Mitchell, Greg, "15 Stories They've Already Bungled," 2003. Online at http://www.editorandpublisher.com/eandp/news/article_display.jsp?vnu_content_id=1850208] (as of August 5, 2003).

[12] PSRA/*Newsweek* poll conducted April 10–11, 2003, n = 1,000, Roper Center at University of Connecticut, *Public Opinion Online*, accessed through Lexis-Nexis (as of July 27, 2004).

[13] Fox News/Opinion Dynamics poll conducted April 8–10, 2003, n = 900, Roper Center at University of Connecticut, *Public Opinion Online*, accessed through Lexis-Nexis (as of July 27, 2004).

rather than overall satisfaction, is considered. For example, one might propose that the embedded press system did a disservice to the public by increasing the risk to "their" soldiers by increasing the risk of violations of operational security. Consider this *Los Angeles Times* poll question (for April 2–3, 2003, n = 745):

> Reporters have been assigned to U.S. military units in the region of **Iraq** and given unprecedented access to military action and personnel. Which of the following statements comes closer to your view? . . . Greater media coverage of the military action and U.S. personnel in **Iraq** is good for the country because it gives the American people an uncensored view of events as they unfold. Greater media coverage of the military action and U.S. personnel in **Iraq** is bad for the country because it provides too much information about military actions as they unfold.
>
> Good for country—55%
> Bad for country—37
> Don't know—8[14]

One could imagine practices specific to certain systems of organizing press-military relations, such as elements of the embedded press system, that, it might be argued, do not leave the public well-served. Alternatively, one could consider practices intrinsic to contemporary styles of reporting and news coverage that are not in the public interest. While an interesting line of inquiry, the implications of general press practices are beyond the scope of this book.

Overall, the embedded press system as implemented in Iraq earned positive marks in all outcomes except operational security. Since these "positive" outcomes are not yet considered relative to anything, the next section attempts to put the embedded press system in historical context and compares the outcomes related to this system, where possible, with those related to the systems used in the other case studies discussed in Chapter Three.

---

[14] *Los Angeles Times* poll conducted April 2–3, 2003, n = 745, Roper Center at University of Connecticut, *Public Opinion Online*, accessed through Lexis-Nexis (as of July 27, 2004).

## Comparison of Embedded Press and Other Systems for Organizing Press-Military Relations

This section presents notional press-military outcomes for each of the cases discussed in Chapter Three relative to the war in Iraq. We begin with a chart that summarizes notional outcomes for all the cases and then spend the balance of the section justifying the values attributed to different outcomes in different cases based on our understanding of the cases themselves.

Table 5.3 presents these notional values of outcomes of different operations. In each cell, a plus (+) denotes a positive, good, or satisfactory outcome; multiple pluses (++) indicate a *more* positive outcome, both in absolute terms and relative to operations with fewer pluses. Minuses (–) denote negative, poor, or insufficient outcomes relative to notional reasonably expected standards. Multiple minuses (––)again indicate particularly negative outcomes. Empty cells indicate either neutral outcomes or outcomes for which we lack sufficient information to make a judgment.

### Military Goals and Measures

**Do Not Allow News Coverage to Compromise Operational Security.** Operational security is best when the press is denied access, or when security review is implemented. In the case studies, we found remarkably few violations of operational security due to press coverage, and no evidence of compromises of operational security. While the embedded press system in Iraq maintained operational security reasonably well relative to the implicit threat of having reporters in units with real-time communication capabilities, several reporters were nonetheless disembedded for violating the security arrangements.

Of particular note was the violation of operational security in Haiti. While operational security during Operation Restore Hope in Haiti was unimportant (since it ended up being a humanitarian intervention), during the 11th-hour diplomatic mission (which ultimately resulted in the abdication of the Haitian dictator), the Haitian

**Table 5.3**
**Notional Values of Measures of Different Operations**

| Outcomes | Vietnam | Grenada | Panama | 1st Gulf War | Somalia | Haiti | Former Yugoslavia | Afghanistan | Iraq |
|---|---|---|---|---|---|---|---|---|---|
| **Military** | | | | | | | | | |
| Operational security | + | ++ | ++ | + | | – | + | + | – |
| Legal obligations | | | | | | | | | |
| Sufficient press access | + | – – – | – | – – | + | + | | | + |
| Public | – | + | + | + | – | – | | + | + |
| Support military mission | | | | | | | | | |
| Good public relations | | | | | | | | | |
| Public informed | – – | – | – | + | – | – | – | | + |
| Press | – | – – | – | – – | + | | | | + |
| International | – | – | – | + | | + | | | – |
| Credibility | – – | – | + | + | – | | | | + |
| Information operations | – – | | | | | | – | | + |
| **Press** | | | | | | | | | |
| Newsworthy information | | | | | | | | | |
| Access | ++ | – – – | – | – | + | ++ | – | – | ++ |
| Safety | – | ++ | +/– | ++ | – | + | + | + | – |
| Provide information to the public | | | | | | | | | |
| 4th Estate obligation | | | | | | | | | |
| Market share | | | | | | | | | |
| Print | | | | | | | | | |
| Television | | | | | | | | | |
| "Quality" journalism | | | | | | | | | |
| Accuracy | | | | | | | | | |
| Credibility | – | | | | | | | | – |
| Public | | | | | | | | | |
| **Gain information** | | | | | | | | | |
| Satisfaction | – | + | + | + | – | | | + | + |
| Informed | – | | | + | | | | – | + |
| Be "well-served" | –/+ | – | – | ? | | | | | ? |

NOTES: A plus (+) denotes a positive, good, or satisfactory outcome; multiple pluses (++) indicate a *more* positive outcome, both in absolute terms and relative to operations with fewer pluses. A plus and minus (+/–) denotes a mixed outcome or pros and cons. Minuses (–) denote negative, poor, or insufficient outcomes relative to notional reasonably expected standards. Multiple minuses again indicate particularly negative outcomes. Empty cells indicate either neutral outcomes or outcomes for which we lack sufficient information to make a judgment. A question mark (?) indicates an outcome that is open to debate depending on the normative stance taken.

**RAND** *MG200-5.3*

military regime learned from a cable news broadcast that U.S. forces were en route to Haiti. Although this report may have played a role in convincing the Haitian military leaders to step down, it also posed great risk to President Carter's negotiating team, who could have been seized as hostages (which would have been an unprecedented compromise of operational security).

**Fulfill Legal Obligations Regarding Press Access.** The recent war in Iraq is unique in that it is the first recent conflict in which the military's twin obligations of informing the public and granting adequate press access were both largely satisfied. In the past, either only one or neither of these obligations were met. For example, in Vietnam, the press had broad access, but the military and the administration kept many secrets from the public, including real estimates of enemy strength, accurate casualties figures, and realistic projections of war progress. In the first Gulf War, the military provided considerable information to the public but failed to allow the press to collect or confirm that information with their own independent findings. Somalia and Haiti both had broad press access, but total volume of coverage and the amount of public attention paid to these operations were low. Scoring these as negatives for the military in Table 5.3 is arbitrary; the bottom line is that the public wasn't well informed about operations in Haiti and Somalia. The extent to which this is the fault of the military, the press, or the members of the public themselves remains unclear.

**Use News Coverage to Support Military Mission.** *Obtain good Public Relations.* In the cases reviewed, the public was found to be generally supportive of the military, although the press was much harder to please. The public is generally supportive of the military during times of conflict; the only combat operation in the case histories that wasn't viewed favorably by the majority of the public was Vietnam. The public is less supportive of humanitarian operations that are outside of core national interests when they cost the lives of American soldiers, as was the case in Somalia.[15]

The press is much harder to please than the public. Public relations with the press align perfectly with press access, unsurprisingly, again, with the exception of Vietnam. Of particular note is the extent to which military public relations with the press and military public relations with the public are divorced from one another. Consider the first Gulf War, in which there was considerable coverage, but mostly from official government/military sources. The public was quite content with the coverage of the first Gulf War (see Table 5.4, below); in fact, public approval of coverage of the first Gulf War was comparable to public approval for coverage of the major combat operations phase of OIF. However, the press was incensed at the restricted access during the first Gulf War and protested vehemently.

*Build credibility.* Historical data make it hard to disentangle administration credibility from military credibility, perhaps because they are conflated in people's minds as well as by the role of the president as "commander in chief." Looking over the cases, it is clear that credibility is tied more to the nature of operations and their justification than to systems of press relations. During Vietnam, many in the press felt that the administration had been deliberately misleading the public. In Grenada, the stated reasons for the invasion had very little to do with reality.[16] However, it is unclear to what extent the public cared. "Mission creep" in Somalia joined by the unexpected U.S. casualties in the "Black Hawk down" incident were a blow to administration credibility. Even in Iraq, where quick victory and positive, credibility-enhancing behavior by the military helped the military's image, misunderstandings about the Jessica Lynch rescue, for example, and the failure (to date) to find weapons of mass destruction may result in overall loss of credibility.

---

[15] Larson, Eric V., *Casualties and Consensus: The Historical Role of Casualties in Domestic Support for U.S. Military Operations*, Santa Monica, Calif.: RAND Corporation, MR-726-RC, 1996.

[16] See the discussion in Paul, *Marines on the Beach*.

*Support information operations.* Certain forms of "honest" information operations are available only in the face of enemy propaganda or disinformation campaigns. Having high levels of press involvement (as in Iraq) allows debunking, while excluded or limited press coverage (as in Kosovo) does not.

In Kosovo, lack of independent media on the ground prevented the debunking of false enemy claims, while during major combat operations in Iraq, the presence of independent media prevented credence being given to false enemy claims. For protection against propaganda and disinformation, systems that allow good relations with the press and reasonable press access (such as embedded press and unilateral press in a permissive environment) are most effective.

## Press Goals and Measures

**Gain Access to Newsworthy Information.** *Establish a satisfactory access arrangement.* Press access is determined by what the military offers, what the military actually provides (a distinction that became clear in Panama, where the military activated the press pool, but then didn't show the pool any combat), what journalists are able to get for themselves, and what kind of access is actually possible, given the nature of operations.

Press access has been best where the military has allowed access to units (Vietnam and Iraq), or where the press has been able to unilaterally *take* access (Somalia and Haiti). Operations that primarily involve air war or special forces afford poor access to operations.

*Ensure reporter safety.* When reporters are kept away from the action, they are safe. In contrast, unilateral journalism is dangerous. Being an embedded journalist is dangerous, but less dangerous than being a unilateral (being surrounded by armed men, all of whom wish to survive, has its advantages). One editor particularly liked the safety factor of the embedded press: "I didn't want my reporters driving around the battlefield during a high intensity conflict looking for stories, because they'll get killed."[17]

---

[17] Quoted in Shafer, "Embeds and Unilaterals."

**Provide Newsworthy Information to the Public.** *Fulfill 4th Estate obligations, build market share.* The extent to which 4th Estate obligations are being met is difficult to determine from case studies. Presumably the press tried to fulfill its 4th Estate obligations in all of these conflicts; even in Vietnam the press eventually began to produce its own independently verified reports. Market share is more a concern of individual press agencies than a concern of the public or an important policy question.

**Maintain Quality of News.** *Maintain fairness, objectivity, and accuracy of news.* Table 5.4 shows public perceptions of media coverage (which relates to quality of coverage) over time. We see that the public found press coverage of both Gulf Wars to be predominantly excellent or good, while the conflicts without a strong conventional forces component receive fewer "excellent" ratings.

As discussed in Chapter Three, it is difficult to cover an air war, and the public perception of coverage of such operations confirms it.

*Build credibility.* Press credibility is difficult to assess without research focusing specifically on that topic. What we have inferred is that press credibility may have taken a blow in Vietnam, when elements of the public became skeptical of both the government's message and those who reported it. Likewise, it is our perception that the credibility of at least some press agencies has suffered somewhat from the war in Iraq: particularly those agencies that perpetrated the "week-two jitters" (see Chapter Three) with their "experts" and agencies whose reporters were ejected from the theater or otherwise accused of misconduct. Whether these incidents actually had any effects on the overall credibility of the press or any kind of durable consequences, even on specific agencies, remains to be seen.

### Public Goals and Measures

**Get Information.** Public satisfaction seems to correlate highly with operational success, at least for combat operations. Public satisfaction with operations other than war is lower in general and dips severely if the costs outweigh the benefits, as was arguably the case in Somalia.

**Table 5.4**
**Relative Media Coverage Ratings**

| Conflict | Poll Date | Excellent | Good | Only Fair | Poor | Don't Know/ No Opinion | Source |
|---|---|---|---|---|---|---|---|
| Iraq | 4/2/03 | 32% | 42% | 15% | 9% | 2% | (1) |
| | 3/29/03 | 38% | 41% | 13% | 7% | 1% | (2) |
| | 3/22/03 | 52% | 32% | 10% | 5% | 1% | (3) |
| | 3/20/03 | 42% | 38% | 11% | 4% | 5% | (4) |
| Afghanistan | 7/8/02 | 25% | 46% | 20% | 7% | 2% | (5) |
| Kosovo | 9/1/99 | 15% | 42% | 26% | 9% | 7% | (6) |
| Bosnia | 9/28/95 | 12% | 49% | 27% | 5% | 7% | (7) |
| | 5/6/93 | 18% | 64% | 10% | 4% | 5% | (8) |
| 1st Gulf War | 1/30/91 | 42% | 37% | 13% | 7% | 1% | (9) |
| | 1/27/91 | 63% | 26% | 8% | 2% | 1% | (10) |

(1) March–April 2003 War Tracking poll conducted April 2–7, 2003, n = 912, Roper Center at University of Connecticut, *Public Opinion Online*, accessed through Lexis-Nexis (as of July 27, 2004).
(2) Gallup/CNN/*USA Today* poll conducted March 29–30, 2003, n = 1,012, Roper Center at University of Connecticut, *Public Opinion Online*, accessed through Lexis-Nexis (as of July 27, 2004).
(3) CNN/*USA Today* poll conducted March 22–23, 2003, n = 1,020, Roper Center at University of Connecticut, *Public Opinion Online*, accessed through Lexis-Nexis (as of July 27, 2004).
(4) "Late March War Tracking" poll conducted March 20–22, 2003, n = 903, Roper Center at University of Connecticut, *Public Opinion Online*, accessed through Lexis-Nexis (as of July 27, 2004).
(5) "People and the Press—Media Update" poll conducted July 8–16, 2002, n = 1,365, Roper Center at University of Connecticut, *Public Opinion Online*, accessed through Lexis-Nexis (as of July 27, 2004).
(6) "News Interest Index" poll conducted September 1–12, 1999, n = 1,205, Roper Center at University of Connecticut, *Public Opinion Online*, accessed through Lexis-Nexis (as of July 27, 2004).
(7) "News Interest Index" poll conducted September 28–October 1, 1995, n = 1,519, Roper Center at University of Connecticut, *Public Opinion Online*, accessed through Lexis-Nexis (as of July 27, 2004).
(8) ABC News poll conducted May 6, 1993, n = 516, Roper Center at University of Connecticut, *Public Opinion Online*, accessed through Lexis-Nexis (as of July 27, 2004).
(9) Gallup poll conducted January 30–February 2, 1991, n = 1,005, Roper Center at University of Connecticut, *Public Opinion Online*, accessed through Lexis-Nexis (as of July 27, 2004).
(10) Gallup poll conducted January 17–20, 1991, n = 1,019, Roper Center at University of Connecticut, *Public Opinion Online*, accessed through Lexis-Nexis (as of July 27, 2004).
NOTE: Percentages are rounded.

The extent to which the public is informed about an operation or is following the operation also depends very little on the system for press-military relations in place, and much more on other factors. Note that Figure 5.1 above shows very high levels of coverage for both Iraq wars, even though the sources of information for much of the first Gulf War reporting were "official" (military and government) sources. While the reporters were upset with their inability to collect or verify their own stories, the public was well-satisfied and paid attention to the news they were provided.

**Seek to Be "Well-Served."** It is very difficult to tell whether the public was well-served by the coverage in any of these cases without making a normative stand on what it means to be "well-served." With that in mind, we recognize a 4th Estate argument that the public can expect to be better served in a case where the press is allowed access and an opportunity to verify the claims of official sources. We also consider valid a normative position that holds that some forms of news coverage may not serve the public good. We discuss this at greater length in Chapter Six in the section on "Technology and the Consequences of the 24-Hour News Cycle."

## Implications for Coverage of Future Conflicts

In this section, we make some observations about different systems of press-military relations by considering the outcomes that might be expected from each of the "pure" strategies for access and operational security discussed in Chapter Four. Table 5.5 presents the expected outcomes of the various access and security strategies if implemented in a generic military operation, given contemporary reporting conditions. In the sections that follow, we discuss factors that, if changed, might be expected to alter those "generic" outcomes.

As in Table 5.3, the pluses in Table 5.5 denote the positive or good outcomes, while minuses are low or poor outcomes. This table produces slightly more nuanced, but comparable views to those expressed in Tables 4.1 and 4.2 in Chapter Four. Table 5.5 suggests

**Table 5.5**
**Generic Expected Outcome Effects from Different Systems of Press-Military Relations**

| Outcomes | Denial of Access | Press Pool | Embedded Press | Unilateral Journalism | Credentials | Security Review |
|---|---|---|---|---|---|---|
| **Military** | | | | | | |
| Operational security | + | + | – | – – | + | ++ |
| Legal obligations | – – | +/– | + | ++ | | – |
| Sufficient press access | – – | – | + | + | + | |
| Public informed | – – | + | ++ | + | | – |
| Support military mission | | | | | | |
| Good public relations | | | | | | |
| Public informed | ← Depends on other factors → | | | | | |
| Press | – – | – | + | + | | – |
| International | ← Depends on other factors → | | | | | |
| Credibility | – | | + | + | | – |
| Information operations | – – | – | + | + | | |
| **Press** | | | | | | |
| Newsworthy information | | | | | | |
| Access | – – | – | + | ++ | | |
| Safety | ++ | + | | – | + | |
| Provide information to the public | | | | | | |
| 4th Estate obligation | | | | | | |
| Market share | | | | | | |
| Print | – | – | + | + | | + |
| Television | – – | – | ++ | ++ | | – |
| "Quality" journalism | | | | | + | + |
| Accuracy | | | | | | |
| Credibility | | | | | | |
| **Public** | | | | | | |
| Gain information | | | | | | |
| Satisfaction | | | | | | |
| Informed | | | | | | – |
| Be "well-served" | – | | | | | +/– |

NOTE: See notes for Table 5.3.
RAND *MG200-5.5*

that, in general, a combination of embedded press and unilateral journalism, like the system of coverage used during major combat operations in Iraq, has favorable or positive outcomes across the board, with the exception of operational security and safety. The addition of a system of credentials (again, like the system as implemented at the beginning of OIF) mitigates the risks to those two outcomes without other ill effects.

## The Consequences of Different Contexts on Press-Military Relations

In addition to the general qualities of the various systems for organizing press-military relations, there are several other factors that might affect important outcomes. Any of these factors could sufficiently change the context or implementation of a system of press-military relations and thereby influence the expected outcomes of that system in the generic case (see Table 5.5).

### Legacies of Previous Conflicts

What has gone before matters. For example, given the successes of the embedded press system in the war in Iraq, the majority of stakeholders from all three constituencies (military, press, and public) will likely expect to see the embedded press system (or something very much like it) used in the next major U.S. military operation. Should that fail to occur because of one or more of the factors below, or some accident or even calculated press policy decision, certain "relationship" outcomes, such as the military's good public relations with the press and the public, are likely to be diminished, simply because of disappointed expectations.

On the other hand, a legacy of shared understanding and professional integrity may reduce the potential for breaches of operational security that might otherwise be expected from systems such as the embedded press.

### Technology

Given the dramatic changes wrought by previous technological innovation such as television and the real-time global coverage made possible by advances in portable satellite-based communications, it isn't impossible that some future innovation will change the nature of coverage and force innovation and change in press-military relations. Technology renders certain systems of press-military relations obsolete; denial of access becomes almost impossible when anyone with a digital camera can produce "footage" that might make its way to the networks. Technology also has important implications for other outcomes, particularly operational security and market share. The Internet in particular is already changing the nature of news, reporting, and coverage.

Between 1995 and 2002, there has been a 32-fold increase in Internet host availability. This trend is much more pronounced than the trend for Internet usage for news. While these data do not show the percentage of the pool of Internet hosts being utilized for news and current events, it does suggest that the Internet is likely to become a more important source of news in the future. Indeed, numerous bloggers have provided first-hand accounts of battles, ostensibly from the eyes of journalists, soldiers, Iraqi exiles, Baghdad residents, and other observers of the war.

### Planning and Lead Time

The amount of lead time for planning and preparation of a system of press-military relations prior to the commencement of an operation can influence the way that system is implemented. Previous research notes the importance of secret versus public and crisis versus premeditated decisional processes in conditioning military intervention decisions.[18] The same factors have the potential to influence the implementation of systems of press-military relations, and thus to influence relevant outcomes. Whether an operation occurs in response to an immediate crisis or to a durable state determines the lead time avail-

---

[18] Paul, Christopher, "The U.S. Military Intervention Decision-Making Process: Who Participates, and How?" *Journal of Political and Military Sociology*, Vol. 32, No. 1, 2004.

able to military planners of press policy. A crisis operation, such as the one in Grenada, left very little time to consider press options, and thus the somewhat self-defeating system of denial of access was imposed. Both the first Gulf War and Operation Iraqi Freedom, however, had reasonably long lead times before the actual operation and afforded planners the opportunity to consider press relations well in advance.

The secrecy of the operation affects the lead time *for the press only*. In a premeditated but secretly planned operation, such as Operation Just Cause in Panama, the military has plenty of time to consider press relations, although the press does not. The absence of reactive press pressure during the planning phase of secret operations makes it easier for military planners to avoid the issue of providing for access or to make plans that will end up being unsatisfactory to the press.

Anything that shortens the time the press has to prepare (either crisis or secrecy) constrains the implementation of certain press systems. For example, for the invasion of Panama, had Pentagon public affairs wanted to embed reporters, it would have been virtually impossible to do so on a large scale without violating the secrecy of the operation. Further, anything that foreshortens the length of potential press pre-participation can create a lack of dialogue between the press and the military because of the constraints on available time in which such dialogue can take place. When a proposed system is discussed, understood, and accepted by both sides prior to the commencement of the operation, success is more likely on more outcomes.

Future plans to implement systems of press-military relations that seem to require extensive preparations, such as embedded press, need to be made with cognizance of the possibility of short lead times before a conflict.

### Nature of the Operation

The nature of the operation (ground war, air war, or operation other than war) can have important effects on several press-military outcomes.

Conventional ground war is the default assumption of all of the different systems of press-military relations. *But if conventional ground forces are not used, coverage becomes more problematic.* Consider, for example, an operation conducted almost exclusively by special forces on the ground (such as the war in Afghanistan). Several factors prevent reporters from covering special operations, including, for example, the following: Some tactics and equipment used by special forces are classified, the missions themselves are often highly sensitive, operational security is even more critical because of the potential vulnerability of small numbers of highly trained troops, troops must travel and operate under difficult conditions, and there is no available support in special forces units for "superfluous" personnel. While it is not unreasonable to limit access to special forces personnel and operations, if such operations comprise *all* operations in theater and no access is provided, several press-military outcomes may suffer.

Other problems arise when a conflict is primarily an air war. There is still no good way to cover an air war. It isn't safe to allow reporters near the targets; it isn't interesting to have reporters in the bombers; it isn't feasible to have reporters in the cockpits of fighters, and it isn't safe to allow reporters to film live at carriers and airstrips (from an operational security point of view). This leaves coverage fragmented and heavily dependent on official footage, which may include the breathtaking but difficult-to-contextualize footage made available from cameras mounted on precision munitions. Reporters needing stories focus on what they can get, which has the potential to be a very incomplete picture of the war. For example, in Bosnia, Operation Allied Force—viewed through the media prism—became a conflict in which

> the individual incident is played up, and the general trend is played down . . . a series of individual newsworthy events, some of which are decisive to the outcome of the conflict, others of which are totally irrelevant.[19]

---

[19] Pounder, "Opportunity Lost," p. 58.

While air war can alter several coverage and access related outcomes, it doesn't have a greatly negative overall effect on press-military relations or related outcomes. This is probably because participants on both sides of the military-media divide recognize that, with current technology, there is no good way to cover an air war.[20]

### Quality of Opposition

In U.S. operations since Vietnam, the quality of the opposition relative to U.S. troops has been "poor" or "marginal" at best. Low-quality opponents gives the military considerable flexibility in planning press-military relations:

> The "enemy" could not seriously challenge the U.S. military. Such overwhelming force in the face of a weak enemy allows the U.S. military more latitude to organize media relations and "experiment" with new, more liberal approaches. That this frame of mind will remain in the face of a more sophisticated enemy or during a politically controversial operation remains to be seen.[21]

As opposition quality increases, several outcomes are highlighted and threatened. Operational security becomes particularly critical for several reasons. First, a higher-quality opponent is more likely to have the means to exploit a compromise in operational security. Knowing something about the location of U.S. headquarters is of no use if the enemy has no assets to strike them with, but it is very useful if it does have those assets. Second, more-sophisticated enemies are more likely to have the analytic resources to turn a media-based violation of operational security into a compromise of operational security. Third, a sufficiently sophisticated enemy may be able to turn the transmissions of a reporter's equipment into a compromise of operational security, independent of the content of the transmissions, by using them to determine the exact location of a reporter, and by generalization, of the troops with whom he or she is embedded.

---

[20] Porch, "No Bad Stories," pp. 85–107.

[21] Combelles-Siegel, *The Troubled Path to the Pentagon's Rules on Media Access to the Battlefield, Grenada to Today*, p. 34.

Likewise, if the opposition is of higher quality, danger to reporters in theater uniformly increases. Reporters under any system of press relations are in greater danger if the enemy is projecting greater lethal force farther. This danger is particularly compounded in the embedded press system, where reporters are targeted much like soldiers are in U.S. military units. In addition, journalists reporting from within units that are destroyed or overrun could produce dramatic footage that could have adverse public relations consequences.

As quality of opposition increases, so does the ability of the opposition to engage in effective propaganda or disinformation campaigns. The presence of such campaigns creates the possibility for a positive (or a negative) outcome. For example, consider the disinformation campaign engendered by the opposition in the former Yugoslavia, where, arguably, U.S. forces engaged the most sophisticated forces of any of the cases mentioned in Chapter Three. The lack of effective independent reporting of the allied air campaign made it very difficult for the allies to credibly deny inflated claims of collateral damage made by the opposition.

In the last instance, genuinely high-quality opposition has quite concerning implications for press-military relations. If the military is really "fighting for all of our lives," then first-order constitutional obligations are likely to overshadow second-order constitutional and legal obligations to a certain extent, likely at the expense of press prerogatives.

### The Value of Victory

The old aphorism, "All's well that ends well," holds more than a little bit of truth with regard to most people's perceptions of wars and war coverage. Operational success and military victory provide very little grist for the mill of unfavorable coverage, and coverage of operational successes is good public relations in its own right. Success and victory leave the public ill-disposed toward complaints from the press about their treatment at the hands of the military. Victory all but assures the military good relations with the public and increases the likelihood of good public relations with press, if coupled with broad access.

> Everyone was lucky the formula worked, and it worked in part because the war was a short one, but if the war had gone on longer, if U.S. casualties had increased, I'm not sure the enthusiasm for the embed process would be as high as it is now in the Pentagon.[22]

## The Price of Failure

In contrast, when things go poorly it can be very taxing on press-military relations, especially if broad access has been granted to the press. Even though the press is "just doing its job," when reports of military failures, mistakes, or disasters go out, they make the military look bad and make members of the military upset.

Systems of press-military relations that allow significant press access, such as the embedded press system, rely heavily on the ability of U.S. forces to successfully complete their missions with a minimum of errors. As the commanding general of the 1st Marine Division in Iraq notes in his lessons learned summary:

> Before we as a collective military society congratulate ourselves on the "overwhelming success" of the embed program, we need to pause and remember that we were both good and lucky. We achieved victory quickly and were successful in keeping our casualties low. We took great pains to limit collateral damage and this paid off in the court of public opinion. The media brings the spotlight to our stage for good and ill. What would have been the headlines if the Coalition lost a battalion of infantrymen in a chemical attack? What if there was more nationalistic spirit in the hearts of the people of Iraq and a majority of the population fought us block-by-block?[23]

---

[22] Marvin Kalb quoted in "Pentagon Ponders Embedded Reporter Policy," *The New York Times*, June 18, 2003.

[23] Mattis, James N. (Commanding General, 1st Marine Division), *Operation Iraqi Freedom (OIF) Lessons Learned,* Washington, D.C.: U.S. Department of Defense, May 29, 2003, p. 33.

Two factors make the cost of failure exceedingly high: first, the expectation of perfection and, second, the hyperbole inherent in modern television news coverage.

Regarding expectations:

> The combination of real-time visual imagery on television coupled with a public conditioned to film of bombs going down ventilator shafts has the public expecting perfection in war—which can never be perfect. This perception, and the media and telecommunications capabilities that helped create it, has the potential to affect significantly the future use of U.S. military force.[24]

Perfection is a difficult standard but a laudable goal. Given the general tendency of news reporting to include the exceptional and the dramatic, mistakes will be publicized, while successes may not. Further, what constitutes "bad news" may not need to be all that bad; consider the "week-two jitters" during the major combat operations phase of OIF (see Chapter Three).

Some of this can be blamed on what has been called the "house-of-mirrors effect": Contemporary battlefield coverage hyperbolizes; that which is good is very, very good; that which is bad is truly horrible.[25] While we wish to argue that the fun-house-mirror effect is inherent in the broader nature of the contemporary news processes, it is certainly visible in the implementation of the embedded press systems. As Shafer notes:

> And while embedded TV journalists beamed back to the studio compelling footage of battlefield bang-bang, the networks failed to place the action in proper context. Exchanges of small-arms fire were inflated into major shootouts by television, and minor (though deadly) skirmishes became full-bore battles. Also, the journalistic tendency to put a human face on every story hyper-

[24] Adamson, *The Effects of Real-Time News Coverage on Military Decision-Making*, p. 9.

[25] Hess, "Pentagon Gamble Pays Off—So Far."

bolized coalition setbacks, such as the ambush of Pfc. Jessica Lynch and her comrades.[26]

## Conclusion

As noted above, our analysis finds that the embedded press system is, in general, likely to produce the greatest number of the most positive outcomes for press-military relations. Note, however, that successful implementation of this system relies on both the press and the military, and it is vulnerable to diminished performance due to many other factors, including limited operational lead time or the nature of the operation.

Nor is the embedded press system to be considered a "sure winner" in all future conflicts. In the final chapter of this book, we consider some potential shortcomings of the embedded press system and discuss other implications of this research.

---

[26] Shafer, "Embeds and Unilaterals."

CHAPTER SIX

# The Future of Embedded Press

> The Pentagon officer who conceived and advanced the embedded journalist program should step forward and demand a fourth star for his epaulets. By prepping reporters in boot camps and then throwing them in harm's way with the invading force, the U.S. military has generated a bounty of positive coverage of the Iraq invasion, one that decades of spinning, bobbing, and weaving at rear-echelon briefings could never achieve.
>
> — Jack Shafer[1]

Having presented our core findings in Chapter Five, we now raise several issues concerning the embedded press system that arose during the course of our research, but that were either not directly related to our main objective of evaluating the embedded press and other systems for military-press relations or are outside the scope of our evaluative framework. After briefly illuminating these issues, we conclude with suggestions for further research.

[1] Shafer, "Embeds and Unilaterals."

## Widespread Applause

The embedded press system has proven to be broadly popular. The embedded press system is

> one of the most remarkable win-win-win propositions. It's clear that journalists, who want access more than anything else, were given remarkable access. It seems to me clear that the military got much more favorable coverage than they would have had had there not been embedding. And it's clear that the public saw a type of picture that they had never, never had an opportunity to see before.[2]

This assessment of the system's broad success is unsurprising, given the positive expected outcomes from the system in general (see Table 5.5) and the favorable outcomes actually realized in Iraq (see Table 5.3 and the discussion in Chapter Five).

This study has found that the embedded press system, when coupled with unilateral reporting and a credentialing system to protect operational security, is expected to result in positive outcomes in almost every category of evaluation that we consider.

## Possible Shortcomings

However, the extent to which these positive outcomes are achieved can be affected by implementation failures (based on planning, lead time, or personalities), operations not conducive to this kind of coverage (special operations and air war), failed operations, or operations against sophisticated enemies.

Moreover, although our analysis found that operational security was the only area in which the embedded press might be expected to have a negative outcome, we also noted several other potential shortcomings. The following discussion will allow us to highlight ways in which future uses of the embedded press might be improved.

---

[2] Brookings, *Assessing Media Coverage of the War in Iraq.*

### The Embedded Press System Created a Hierarchy of Credentials

Making embedded reporters the only "official" reporters relegates unilateral reporters to the status of second-class citizens in the combat theatre. As Shafer notes,

> One troubling side effect of the program was that it created a credentialing system among reporters: The embedded were considered official journalists, to whom the military would generally talk, and the unilaterals were often treated as pests with no right to the battlefield. In many instances, the military prevented unilaterals from covering the war, especially in the southern cities left in the invasion's wake: Basra, Umm Qasr, Nasiriyah, and Safwan.[3]

Given that the press system implemented in Iraq was actually embedded press plus unilaterals and that many observers have applauded the contribution of the unilateral reporters to an otherwise narrow view of the war, *future systems would do well to consider credentialing and validating unilateral reporters to some extent.* Unilateral reporting also has largely favorable outcomes, as discussed in Chapter Five.

### The "Soda-Straw" View of War

While embedded coverage is potentially very "deep" and detailed, it is unlikely to be broad by its nature. The view reported by journalists embedded in line units is by nature a fairly narrow view; the opposite of "the big picture" and accused by many of being what General Richard Myers, Chairman of the Joint Chiefs, has called "the soda-straw view of war."[4] Embedded reporters can reliably report only what they have seen, though they can report that narrow view with great detail.

But any soda-straw effect can be mitigated by combining numerous soda straws to create a large picture. However, rather than providing the public with a "fly eye" fractal view of this larger picture

---

[3] Shafer, "Embeds and Unilaterals."

[4] Council on Foreign Relations, *Embedded Journalists in Iraq.*

by providing all of the soda straws directly from the embedded reporters, editors or producers can synthesize the multiple views into more easily digestible reports.

Regardless of how reports from embedded journalists are combined, *embedding should continue to be supplemented by other systems of access that provide access to other sources of information.*

### Loss of Objectivity

One of the recurring themes in the reflexive press discourse surrounding the embedded press system is the implicit threat to journalists' impartiality and neutrality. One journalist has even argued that the term "embed" suggests that the reporter is "in bed" with the military.[5]

> All of the embeds have a strong stake in the outcome of any hostile action they might encounter, hence their understandably enthusiastic embrace of the plural pronouns "we," "our," and "us" to describe the progress of the units to which they're attached. You'd probably use the same words if you were dune-buggying your way to Baghdad.[6]

The psychological phenomenon in which hostages begin to identify with, excuse, and in some cases even actively protect their captors is called "the Stockholm syndrome." While this term is not wholly applicable to the embedded press, there is little doubt that similar pressures are placed on embedded reporters. From the military's perspective, journalists' identification with soldiers can be beneficial since it increases the likelihood of good public relations. But from the perspective of journalists and the public, this closeness can be somewhat alarming.

Journalists can protect themselves from identifying too closely with their assigned units by relying on their professionalism. Several embedded journalists (including one whom we interviewed) admit to

[5] Project for Excellence in Journalism, *Embedded Reporters.*

[6] Shafer, "Embeds and Unilaterals."

having become close to the soldiers in "their" units, relating to them and becoming attached to them. However, all insist that if they had witnessed "their boys" doing something wrong and newsworthy, their professional integrity would win out every time.

Given the myriad pressures and possible sources of bias that are brought to bear on reporters everyday, we do not consider the potential bias inherent in the embedding process to be of too great concern. However, others are concerned by it, and further research may be warranted.

### Technology and the Consequences of the 24-Hour News Cycle

In Chapter Five we refer to the possible fun-house-mirror effect produced by the embedded press, in which that which is good is reported to be fantastic, and that which is bad is reported to be horrific. While we lack data to make a strong claim, we would like to consider the possibility that the fun-house-mirror effect is less a property unique to embedded press, and more properly inherent to the contemporary mode of near-continuous live news coverage, generally referred to as the "24-hour news cycle."

While this innovation in coverage can lead to hyperbole, it also opens up the possibility of increased micromanagement from higher-level commanders based on information made immediately available on television, and it increases pressure on higher-level decisionmakers to make and push decisions down the chain of command at greater speed than ever before:

> An odd new phenomenon occurs with real-time capability. The public now gets credible, current information with commentary from analysts during military operations. In all but the most recent conflicts, this type of information was only available to government and military decision-makers. Now the public gets enough immediate information to form opinions and make decisions of its own. Also, since global commercial television shows no partiality, the enemy has access to the same analyses and intelligence information. And, at a speed which compels political and military authorities to respond quicker and at a frequency

> with which they formerly never had to cope. Real-time news compresses the decision-cycle.[7]

In our view, this pressure on senior decisionmakers to make quick decisions based on partial information without due consideration is a real concern for decisionmakers and field commanders alike.

### Professionalism and Preparation of the Media

Even when bolstered with a system of credentials, operational security from embedded reporters depends on the integrity and professionalism of the reporters: integrity to choose to abide by the terms of their credentialing agreement and professionalism to recognize situations that constitute threats to operational security in the first place. Professionalism and preparation are likely to be inadequate in some regards in a situation in which, for example, a veteran war correspondent complains that many new war correspondents "don't know a tank from a turd."[8]

One of the major principles contained the DoD *Principles for News Media Coverage of DoD Operations,* which followed the first Gulf War, is that news organizations should make their best efforts to assign experienced journalists to combat operations and to make them familiar with U.S. military operations. To the best of our knowledge, this principle has not received serious attention from the news agencies, a view shared by other researchers.[9]

## Suggestions for Future Research

This research has also shown the utility of a systematic and quantitative approach to the evaluation of wartime press-military relations. At the same time, our findings also highlight the value of historical nar-

[7] Adamson, *The Effects of Real-Time News Coverage on Military Decision-Making,* p. 5.

[8] Unidentified correspondent quoted in Andrews, "The Media and the Military," p. 84.

[9] See for example Aukofer and Lawrence, *America's Team*; Pounder, "Opportunity Lost."

rative approaches to problems of this kind. We urge further research in both directions.

We advocate further historical work that focuses on the measurements we identified in Chapter Four. We encourage subject area or case specialists to evaluate their cases using the system of outcomes discussed here.

The preliminary evaluation of the embedded press system contained in this book could be expanded upon with further research on press-military relations in Iraq that captures the experiences and opinions of soldiers and reporters while events are still relatively fresh. Surveys and interviews of the press and the military could make a valuable contribution to the understanding and evaluation of the embedded press system.

In this same vein, further work on the "relations" aspect of press-military relations, especially on the military side, could make an important contribution to this area of study. While our findings suggest that the military (in a monolithic sense) was well-served (in a goals-and-outcomes sense) by the embedded press system, we don't know how most soldiers and officers felt about it. Given our findings regarding the importance of the role of personality, and the importance of informal perceptual legacies in forming the opinions and preferences of future leaders, the personal experiences of junior officers now will likely form and inform the feelings of the high command of the future. Interviews and surveys of military personnel with experience with embedded reporters could provide a very different and very important perspective.

APPENDIX A

# The Public's "Right to Know"

There is an extensive literature on the public's right to know. One body of work takes the position that the public's right to know is a constitutional right. Kent Cooper (former executive director of the Associated Press), who is often credited with coining the term "right to know," stated as early as 1945 that "the citizen is entitled to have access to news, fully and accurately presented. There cannot be political freedom in one country, or in the world, without respect for the 'right to know.'"[1] Cooper writes later, in a book entitled *The Right to Know*, that the First Amendment should be rewritten as "Congress shall make no law . . . abridging the Right to Know through the oral or printed word or any other means of communicating ideas or intelligence."[2] Alexander Meiklejohn ruminates on this more philosophically and holds that the First Amendment rights are justifiable only after establishing the rights of citizens to receive and obtain information: "The First Amendment does not protect a 'freedom to speak.' It protects the freedom of those activities of thought and communication by which we 'govern.'"[3] Others like Wallace Parks (another legal

---

[1] Quoted in O'Brien, David M., *The Public's Right to Know: The Supreme Court and the First Amendment*, New York: Praeger, 1981, p. 2.

[2] Cooper, Kent, *The Right to Know,* New York: Farrar, Straus and Cudahy, 1956, p. 16.

[3] Cited in Foerstel, Herbert N., *Freedom of Information and the Right to Know: The Origins and Applications of the Freedom of Information Act*, Westport, Conn.: Greenwood Press, 1999, p. 11.

scholar and staff attorney for the House Government Affairs Committee) interpreted Meiklejohn's ideas this way:

> It is clear that the primary purpose of the freedom of speech and press clause of the First Amendment was to protect the government from interfering with the communication of facts and views about governmental affairs, in order that all could properly exercise the rights and responsibilities of citizenship in a free society. This clause was intended as one of the guarantees of the people's right to know. It is certainly reasonable to conclude that freedom of the press and speech under contemporary conditions includes the right to gather information from government agencies and stands as a constitutional prohibition against all forms of withholding information beyond that reasonably required for the exercise of delegated power or the protection of other rights.[4]

James Wiggins presents an interesting way to conceptualize the public's right to know by suggesting that it is a combination of the right to

- get information
- print without prior restraint
- print without fear of reprisal not under due process
- access facilities and material essential to communication
- distribute information without interference by government acting under law or by citizens acting in defiance of the law.[5]

Although the First Amendment does not explicitly mention the "right to know," Harold Cross argues that the language of the First Amendment is broad enough to embrace, if not require,

> the inclusion of a right of access to information of government without which the freedom to print could be fettered into futil-

---

[4] Quoted in Foerstel, *Freedom of Information and the Right to Know*, p. 11.

[5] Wiggines, James Russell, *Freedom or Secrecy*, New York: Oxford University Press, 1956, pp. 3–4.

> ity. The history of struggle for freedom of speech and of the press bars any notion that the men of 1791 intended to provide for freedom to disseminate such information but to deny freedom to acquire it.[6]

And what did our founding fathers intend? Looking at James Madison's statement on this issue,

> a popular government, without popular information or the means of acquiring it, is but a Prologue to a Farce or a Tragedy; or perhaps, both. Knowledge will forever govern ignorance: And a people who mean to be their own Governors must arm themselves with the power which knowledge gives.[7]

Clearly, the discussion here relates the constitution to the principles of democratic governance, and it seems to be the case that the right to know is central to the reason for having the First Amendment.

If what Harold Cross states about the broadness of the language in the First Amendment is correct, it is left to the courts and the legal system to determine the boundaries by which the claim on the right to know is legitimate. As Foerstel notes, *Martin v. City of Struthers* (1943) is the first recognition for the right to receive information—as stated in Justice Hugo Black's decision, the First Amendment "freedom embraces the right to distribute literature, and necessarily protects the right to receive it. [Since the right to receive information is] vital to the preservation of a free society."[8] Other majority opinion in *Lamont v. Postmaster General* (1965), *Griswold v. Connecticut* (1965), *Stanley v. Georgia* (1969), *Red Lion Broadcasting Co. v. FCC* (1974), and *Virginia State Board of Pharmacy v. Virginia Citizens Consumer Council* (1976) all upheld the public's right to know.

However, not all court decisions are as accommodating. In fact, in *Zemel v. Rusk* (1965), Chief Justice Earl Warren states that

---

[6] Cross, Harold L., *The Right to Know: Legal Access to Public Records and Proceedings*, New York: Columbia University Press, 1976, pp. 2, 23–24.

[7] Madison, James, *Writings of James Madison*, Vol. 9, New York: Putnam, 1910, p. 103.

[8] Cited in Foerstel, *Freedom of Information and the Right to Know*, pp. 12–13.

> there are few restrictions on action which could not be clothed by ingenious arguments in the garb of decreased data flow. For example, the prohibition of unauthorized entry into the White House diminishes the citizen's opportunities to gather information he might find relevant to his opinion of the way the country is being run, but that does not make entry into the White House a First Amendment right. The right to speak in public does not carry with it the unrestrained right to gather information.

In cases during wartimes, for instance, the court seems to uphold the view that the press does not have the right to print anything it wants [e.g., *Frohwerk v. United States* (1919), *Abrams v. United States* (1919), and *Schenck v. United States* (1919)]. Indeed, O'Brien points out, recognition of a right does not necessarily imply that an individual has the right to exercise that right on all instances—

> claims to a right to know must be linked to the individual's *need to know* about the affairs and operations of government, but in a more specific way than the general claim that an informed citizenry is essential to a representative democracy [emphasis in the original].[9]

Edward Levi puts it this way:

> the people's right to know cannot mean that every individual or interest group may compel disclosure of the papers and effects of government officials whenever they bear on public business. Under our Constitution, the people are the sovereign, but they do not govern by the random and self selective interposition of private citizens.[10]

Herbert Foerstel foresees three possible ways in which the courts can decide on cases involving the public's right to know: The lowest level would prevent the government from interfering with the communication of facts and views about government affairs to the public;

---

[9] O'Brien, *The Public's Right to Know,* p. 14.

[10] Cited in O'Brien, *The Public's Right to Know,* p. 14.

the second level would bind/obligate the government to satisfy public demand for information; and the highest level would impose an affirmative obligation on the government to inform the public. The court, thus far, has not made any decisions confirming the highest level of the right to know or affirming the constitutionally enforceable right of access to government information. Only the lowest level is widely accepted, and it seems to be the case that the courts would need to determine when the right to know trumps or must be subjugated under the public's need to know. As O'Brien points out,

> an individual's interest in knowing, or need to know, entitles that person to claim a right to know when governmental disclosure is vital to that person's self-governance. An individual's need to know is sufficiently meritorious only when demonstrated by a personal or proprietary interest in claiming access to government information.[11]

Another set of topics that emerges in the literature on the concept of the right to know takes a political spin. In particular, the critics of the press lament that the claimant of the public's right to know is different from the supposed recipient of this right. In other words, the claimant of this right (i.e., the press), more often than not, is not the same individual as the supposed beneficiary (i.e., the public) of this right: The "individual" who invokes this claim is often the press, even though the right is supposedly conferred on the people. As William Hocking stated in *Freedom of the Press: A Framework of Principle*: The members of the press "say recklessly that [the public has] a 'right to know'; yet it is a right which they are helpless to claim, for they do not know that they have the right to know what as yet they do not know."[12] In one of the lower court decisions, a judge noted that

> the so called "right of the public to know" is a rationalization developed by the fourth estate to gain rights not shared by others

---

[11] O'Brien, *The Public's Right to Know*, p. 14.

[12] Hocking, William, *Freedom of the Press: A Framework of Principle*, Chicago, Ill.: University of Chicago, 1947, pp. 170–171.

> . . . to improve its private ability to acquire information which is a raw asset of its business. . . . The constitution does not appoint the fourth estate the spokesmen of the people. The people speak through the elective process and through the individuals it elects to positions created for that purpose. The press has no right that exceeds that of other citizens.[13]

In essence then, it seems that the debate comes down to the right to know versus the need to know—one may argue that the public has the right to know what it needs to know in order to govern in a democratic state. What exactly the public needs or does not need to know will depend on the circumstances of the cases and the surrounding context. It seems clear that the members of the public do not have the right to know everything in order to govern/participate effectively because they do not need to know everything to do these things. Thus, in actual practice with regard to military activities, before the law, the military has wide latitude for controlling press access versus claims of "right to know." Because there is no easily discernable threshold for legitimate claims of right to know versus the need to know, exactly what the military's "legal obligations" are in this arena is not easily specified. However, while the threshold is hard to precisely elucidate, gross violations of right to know are not. This creates a situation in which the military, despite extreme practical latitude, is under pressure to allow some "reasonable" level of access to information in service of the right to know in order to avoid a legal challenge at an untenable extreme.

---

[13] Quoted in O'Brien, *The Public's Right to Know,* p. 10.

APPENDIX B

# Outcomes and Measures of the Embedded Press System

> What must astonish people with casual beliefs in the vast power of the media is how difficult it is to measure media influence.
>
> — Michael Schudson[1]

This appendix describes and discusses the specific means of data collection specified as appropriate to the measures/outcomes in Table 4.3. The discussion is explicitly methodological; as we examine each outcome, we consider different ways in which that outcome could be measured. Each discussion concludes with a brief description of the extent to which existing data sources would allow measurement of that outcome, or whether further research requires cultivation of new data sources.

## Measuring the Attainment of Military Outcomes

### Do Not Allow News Coverage to Compromise Operational Security

As an outcome, operational security can be considered in two ways:

- First, as *violations* of operational security—occasions where news coverage reveals something "important" about troops or opera-

[1] Schudson, *The Power of News*, p. 22.

tions that may not already be known to the enemy (e.g., precise or general location), specific tactics, unit identities, intentions, capabilities, strength in force, armaments, and casualty levels).

- Second, as a *compromise* of operational security, where not only is important information broadcast or otherwise released, but the enemy takes advantage of this information to alter his battle plan.[2]

Operational security is difficult to measure for two main reasons. First, the media is not the only source of possible violations of operational security but rather just one potential resource in a vast array of possible enemy intelligence-gathering practices. Second, it is virtually impossible to distinguish enemy action that results from violations of operational security (e.g., an enemy ambush, stiffer defense, or artillery targets based on news broadcast) from that resulting from coincidence in preplanned enemy activities (the ambush or forces might have already been in place or an enemy forward observer might have seen U.S. positions directly without recourse to the news). Unless enemy combatants admit after the fact that they took advantage of a certain security violation or unless U.S. intelligence services intercept enemy transmissions that indicate a violation in operational security and a response to it, the independent effects of media security violations are virtually impossible to discern.

Violations of operational security can be captured through at least three measures. One measure would be *the number of actions cancelled, changed, or postponed because of violations of operational security.* Elements within the military conduct internal monitoring of news coverage for many reasons, keeping an eye out for violations of operational security. A violation or possible compromise of security might result in changes to operational plans. We don't know if mili-

[2] For example, as noted in Andrews, "The Media and the Military," p. 80, Civil War Union General Sherman "was forced to fight a battle he had hoped to avoid at Goldsboro when the Confederate general William Hardee read in the *New York Tribune* that that was where the Yankees were heading." The *New York Tribune* violated Union operational security and Hardee compromised the operation.

tary records presently contain sufficient information to identify actions affected in this way, but if measuring this outcome is of interest to the military, it could certainly arrange to collect data for the measure in future conflicts.

A second measure for violations of operational security might be *the number of reporters whose credentials were revoked or who were chastised for violation of their credentialing agreement.* This measure relies on the same starting logic as for the first measure, elements of the military monitoring news broadcasts and identifying violations of operational security. In an environment where reporters have agreed not to broadcast certain kinds of information, if they are seen to do so, they can be chastised or dismissed. This measure is potentially problematic to the extent that disembedding or revocation of credentials may not be done centrally but may be enforced inconsistently and at lower levels, as was arguably the case in Iraq.[3]

A third and final possible measure of operational security violations would be through careful case analysis. Starting with possible cases identified because of loss of credentials or changes in action plans, interviews, histories, and military records could be used to assemble a careful case study of one or more operational security episodes and to better analyze the consequences of apparent violations.

Regarding the availability of data for these measures, none of the proposed measures can be constructed from existing data bases. Credentials revoked and accounts of the events that occasioned revocation can be gathered from news accounts. Details regarding changes in operational plans are likely classified and will remain unavailable unless the DoD wishes to engage in scrutiny of itself. Detailed case analyses would require interviews of witnesses and/or participants in those events.

### Fulfill Legal Obligations Regarding Press Access

**Press Given Sufficient Access.** To measure the extent to which the press was granted the access it required, we recommend two strate-

[3] One of the reporters we interviewed opined that disembedding was usually handled by the commanding officer at the battalion level, leading to inconsistencies in enforcement.

gies: One is to count access related lawsuits; the other is to conduct content analysis, either "soft" or "topical." This might involve simply looking at the number of articles complaining about access, or engaging in a more in-depth content analysis examining both the frequency and content of press complaints related to access. Given the vagueness before the law of what the military's "obligations" actually are, a measure that considers the satisfaction or dissatisfaction of those to whom the military is "obligated" is preferable. These kinds of data have never been compiled, though the necessary source material (legal records and reflexive reporting) are readily available.

**Public Informed.** Public opinion data about satisfaction with coverage and/or percentage of the general public following an issue can be used to measure the extent to which the public is informed. Questions from public opinion surveys such as Gallup or PSRA might provide good measures. For example, consider the following question: In general, how would you rate the job the press has done in covering the war in _______ . . . excellent, good, only fair or poor? Question wording might be made even more general in order to see how the public views the media during peacetime, for example: In general, how much trust and confidence do you have in the mass media—such as newspapers, TV, and radio—when it comes to reporting the news fully, accurately, and fairly . . . a great deal, a fair amount, not very much, or none?

Some progress could be made on quantifying the extent to which the public was informed based on existing polls. Optimally, research in this area would conduct its own polls/surveys, with questions carefully worded to capture this issue and other measures relevant to this analysis.

### Use News Coverage to Support Military Mission

**Obtain Good Public Relations.** The military wants good public relations with the public, for morale, troop support, and policy support. The military wants good public relations with the press, to encourage positive coverage, minimize complaints, and as evidence that it is meeting its legal obligations.

As an outcome, what is "good" public relations? For the military, it can reasonably be divided into two major strands: regard for the institution of the military and regard for the conduct of the specific military operation. With these two broad outcomes and three discernable audiences (the public, the press, and international publics), measures are fairly straightforward. Public opinion data regarding both the military in general and a specific operation provide reasonable measures of public relations for both domestic and international publics. Between 1971 and 2001, the percentage of people having a great deal of confidence in the military increased from 27 percent to 44 percent.[4] In January 2002, 71 percent of people in a Harris poll reported a "great deal of confidence in the military."[5] On the issue of the recent war and the support for the troops, the Gallup poll (March 29–30, 2003) asked this follow-up question to those who had indicated support for the war:

> Which comes closer to your view of why you favor the war—you think it is the right thing for the U.S. to do and you want to show support for the U.S. troops in Iraq or you are not sure if it is the right thing to do, but you want to show support for the U.S. troops in Iraq.[6]

Different and more careful wording, as in Table B.1—an example from a *Los Angeles Times* poll (for April 2–3, 2003)—can add more detail and nuance than what the Gallup captured.

---

[4] Harris Survey conducted August 1971, n = 1,600, Roper Center at University of Connecticut, *Public Opinion Online*, accessed through Lexis-Nexis (as of July 27, 2004), and Harris poll conducted January 11–15, 2001, n = 1,011, Roper Center at University of Connecticut, *Public Opinion Online*, accessed through Lexis-Nexis (as of July 27, 2004).

[5] Harris poll conducted January 16–21, 2002, n = 1,011, Roper Center at University of Connecticut, *Public Opinion Online*, accessed through Lexis-Nexis (as of July 27, 2004).

[6] Gallup/CNN/*USA Today* poll conducted March 29–30, 2003, n = 1,012, Roper Center at University of Connecticut, *Public Opinion Online*, accessed through Lexis-Nexis (as of July 27, 2004).

**Table B.1**
**Public Opinion Data—Reasons for Support of Iraq War[a]**

| First response | Percentage |
|---|---|
| Disarm Saddam Hussein/Has weapons of mass destruction | 17 |
| Install democratic government in Iraq | 2 |
| Iraq supports terrorists/Terrorism/Al Qaeda | 6 |
| Liberate Iraqi people | 10 |
| Remove threat of attack on America by Iraq | 6 |
| Retaliate for 9/11 [September 11, 2001] terrorist attacks [on the World Trade Center and the Pentagon] | 6 |
| Stabilize the Middle East | 2 |
| Stand behind President [George W.] Bush | 8 |
| Support the troops/patriotism | 3 |
| Saddam Hussein didn't abide by U.N. resolutions | 7 |
| World will be a safer place | 2 |
| Saddam Hussein is evil/His human rights abuses | 9 |
| Finish off 1991 Gulf War | 6 |
| Control of oil resources | |
| Remove Saddam Hussein dictatorship | 1 |
| It's [the war is] the right thing to do | 1 |
| Other | 2 |
| No particular reason/Just support | 11 |
| Not sure | 1 |
| Refused | less than 0.5 |

SOURCE: *Los Angeles Times* poll conducted April 2–3, 2003, n = 745, Roper Center at University of Connecticut, *Public Opinion Online*, accessed through Lexis-Nexis (as of July 27, 2004).

[a]Question: What is the main reason why you support the Bush administration's decision to take military action against Iraq? . . .

Good public relations might also be measured by attitudinal research through well-timed surveys. Such an approach would be particularly appropriate if the wording or methods of existing public opinion research aren't quite right.[7]

[7] The current public opinion data on this issue lacks relevance to the variable of interest. That is, while we may be interested in knowing about the public's opinion about the military as a result of its engagement in a particular military operation, we do not have data that pertain to this question directly. In effect, we have to infer what the public feels about the military as a result of its performance in the operation by looking at what the public feels about the military before and after the operation. Sometimes, these public opinion data are taken

Finally, to measure military public relations regarding reporters, two strategies suggest themselves: first, a survey of reporters (possibly in tandem with a survey of the public with many questions in common) and, second, content analysis similar to that proposed for legal obligations, looking either for generally negative coverage[8] or reporter complaints.

To summarize, existing public opinion poll data can provide a good initial cut at public relations for domestic and international publics, but new survey work could focus questions more precisely on the outcome of interest. To capture public relations with the press, new surveys or analysis of reflexive press writing/reporting would be required.

**Build Credibility.** Credibility measures could be separated into credibility with the public, the press, and internationally, just as with public relations above. In fact, some of the same measures are appropriate: Some existing public opinion surveys ask questions about government or military credibility. Several appropriate questions have already been asked in public opinion research. Take this survey question asked by Public Opinion Dynamics and Fox News on March 25–26 and April 8–9:

> How much do you **trust** the Pentagon to tell the whole truth about the U.S. (United States) **military's** progress in the war with Iraq? . . . A lot, some, not much, not at all?

Another example would be survey research of the kind done through the National Credibility Index (see Table B.2). An approach like the NCI has the advantage of allowing comparisons among groups (for example, between the press and the military). If done repeatedly over time (which has not yet occurred with the NCI), a comparative trend analysis could be very revealing.

---

when the trail has become cold or as the trail is forming—long after the operation or during the military operation, neither of which are immediately after the end of the operation.

[8] Negative coverage could result from confounding negative events, such as battlefield losses, etc. On the whole, one would expect more "negative" coverage of a losing or unsuccessful war than a winning war, even if military relations with the press are otherwise positive.

**Table B.2**
**Credibility Ratings for Sources of Information on Using Military Force in Foreign Affairs**

| Information Source | Rating |
|---|---|
| Military affairs expert | 81.2 |
| Secretary of Defense | 80.4 |
| Chairman, Joint Chiefs of Staff | 80.4 |
| Foreign policy expert | 79.0 |
| High military officer | 77.7 |
| National security advisor | 75.5 |
| Secretary of State | 74.4 |
| U.S. United Nations ambassador | 74.4 |
| Member of the armed forces | 72.5 |
| Representative of national veterans group | 71.4 |
| U.S. president | 69.6 |
| U.S. vice president | 69.3 |
| U.S. senator | 67.1 |
| U.S. congressman | 66.3 |
| Representative of a human rights organization | 57.0 |
| National religious leader | 55.5 |
| Major newspaper/magazine reporter | 53.2 |
| National civil rights leader | 52.6 |
| National syndicated columnist | 52.2 |
| Local religious leader | 51.9 |
| Ordinary citizen | 51.4 |
| TV network anchor | 51.0 |
| Student activist | 36.9 |
| TV/radio talk show host | 35.6 |
| Famous entertainer | 27.6 |

SOURCE: Public Relations Society of America, "Credibility Ratings for Sources of Information on Using Military Force in Foreign Affairs," *The National Credibility Index,* New York, September 1998. See http://www.prsa.org/_About/prsafoundation/nciIndex.asp?ident=prsa0 (as of February 4, 2004).

NOTE: Survey size was 1,501.

Since the NCI is not, at present, a recurring survey, some progress toward effectively quantifying this outcome could be made with existing polls, but, again, new survey work asking questions pertinent to measuring credibility would be optimal.

**Support Information Operations.** According to joint doctrine, information operations are "Actions taken to affect adversary information and information systems while defending one's own information and information systems."[9] Three outcomes are of particular interest: success in protecting oneself from enemy propaganda and disinformation campaigns; success at deceiving the enemy;[10] and success in providing truthful information to the enemy for the purpose of "shock and awe."

Defining "success at deception" as an outcome is particularly difficult; measuring it, even more so. We decline to suggest a measure of successful deception-based information operations. For our purposes, information operations as they relate to the press are efforts either to expose and exploit the truth or are efforts at deception. The military needs to tread very cautiously when considering using the press to disseminate information that is knowingly false or that attempts to mislead. The long-term costs in credibility and poor press relations are likely to outweigh any short-term strategic advantage if the falsehood comes to light; moreover, the press takes great umbrage at the possibility of being "used" to perpetrate an intentional falsehood.

However, when the content of information operations is truthful (e.g., shock and awe), the media is an ideal vehicle. Again, however, the success of "shock and awe" is difficult to measure. Perhaps surveys among former enemy combatants could reveal the effects of intimidation, but it would remain difficult to disentangle the effects of media-conveyed information from intimidation resulting from information from other sources (reputation or first-hand observation).

One desired outcome of information operations is the defeat of enemy propaganda. This might be measured through a content analysis of news coverage focused on news reports that "debunk" enemy

---

[9] *DOD Dictionary of Military and Associated Terms*, Joint Publication 1-02, Washington, D.C.: Joint Chiefs of Staff, as amended through 09 June 2004.

[10] See Gerwehr, Scott, and Russell W. Glenn, *The Art of Darkness: Deception and Urban Operations*, Santa Monica, Calif.: RAND Corporation, MR-1132-A, 2000, for an example of the military application of deception.

claims. Again, this is problematic in that, while it may be possible to measure successful counter-propaganda (debunking of false claims), it is unclear if, in the absence of debunking, this indicates that there was no enemy propaganda, or just no debunking of it.

Measuring the defeat of enemy propaganda is another case where thick detail in rich histories may prove to be a better indicator. For example, in Kosovo, Milosevic went to great lengths to make it appear as if the allied bombing campaign resulted mostly in civilian casualties and high levels of collateral damage. Independent media were not present and were thus unable to confirm or support allied counterclaims. However, in the recent war in Iraq, ludicrous claims by the Iraqi Minister of Information about the effectiveness of Iraqi resistance in Um Qasr were immediately debunked by independent media (i.e., *USA Today*) involved in the extensive media coverage.

Existing databases do not support research on the extent to which press coverage supported information operations. Further, data could be difficult to collect, based on some of the difficulties enumerated above.

## Measuring the Attainment of Press Outcomes

### Gain Access to Newsworthy Information

**Satisfactory Access Arrangement.** Clearly the military can only be expected to allow access to information that they themselves have access to. What isn't clear is what "access" denotes as an outcome, or how to measure it. What is "enough" access? How does one compare access levels between conflicts if the type of access was fundamentally different?

While we don't pretend to have a definitive answer, we do have two thoughts on how to treat access as an outcome, neither of which is particularly satisfying. The first is to rely on journalists' "sense" of access. This is predicated on the assumption that the press knows what good access is, and what is reasonable given the circumstances. Journalists could be surveyed about the access they were allowed following (or even during) hostilities. Clearly journalists' perception of access measures *something* related to access, as do numbers and types of reporting opportunities provided for by the military.

In the same vein, a second approach is to enumerate types of access and consider what access was made available to reporters. One measure would be a simple count of different reporters generating stories based on different sources of information. Content analysis seems appropriate here. Of course access "made available" is different from "available access accepted"—the latter is closer to what is actually measured in the proposed content analysis. Also unconsidered is the general level of interest in unfolding events (determinant of the number of reporters seeking access) and the newsworthiness of events themselves; if a reporter has complete access to something uninteresting, he or she won't generate many news stories about it.

There are no "off the shelf" quantitative measures for the evaluation of access. Existing reflexive press material/reporting should allow for the assembly of qualitative assessments of this outcome.

**Safety of Reporters.** Hand in hand with access is the safety of reporters as they cover a conflict. This is another outcome that is easier to measure in the negative; evidence of failed safety, such as numbers killed or wounded, is an appropriate measure. Taken in ratio with the number of reporters in theater, or with number of soldiers in theater, and controlled for duration of conflict, this measure seems promising. Possible weaknesses include the fact that casualty counts conflate situational danger particular to the conflict (all conflicts are not equally dangerous to reporters) with precautions taken by reporters. These could be teased out with detailed consideration of the actual cases of injury to reporters; such case studies could either retain their character as thick description and become part of a larger narrative or be coded and quantified based on the details of the event.

Reporter injuries and fatalities are available from the Committee to Protect Journalists (http://www.cpj.org/, as of June 18, 2004). Detailed case studies of injury to reporters could require considerable research investment.

### Provide Newsworthy Information to the Public

**Fulfill 4th Estate Obligations.** Since it is impossible to "know everything" and thus determine whether the press is doing an adequate job ferreting out information and presenting it to the public, we cannot rely on content analysis. Instead we must determine public satisfaction with the extent to which the press is performing its 4th Estate obligations, an outcome based on the public's perception rather than on some unobservable qualities of the news content itself. Public perception can be measured through public opinion polls asking questions about satisfaction with coverage, like the questions asked in the polls displayed in Figure 5.2 and Table 5.4.

**Build Market Share.** Networks and publishers already have metrics to measure market share; for print, circulation, and for television, ratings. Nielsen Media Research collects television ratings and sells reports on its results.

### Maintain Quality of News

**Fairness, Objectivity, and Accuracy.** "Quality" in journalism is yet another outcome that is difficult to corral. There is considerable debate over what constitutes quality in journalism. Quality is recognized through various journalistic prizes, but lack of quality is not similarly flagged.

The number of erroneous stories is a clear indicator of lack of quality. Likewise a content analysis of news sources, topics, and style of reporting, like the one recently done by the PEJ, could capture several elements that contribute to the assessment of quality. The PEJ report considers whether stories are primarily factual or interpretive in nature, whether broadcasts had been edited, whether sources of information were provided with the information, etc.[11]

**Credibility.** Called the "coin of the realm" of journalists, credibility is a key goal (see Chapter Two). As an outcome, credibility has as much to do with perception as it does with actually being right, or admitting wrong. Thus, it can be measured either by looking at peo-

---

[11] Project for Excellence in Journalism, *Embedded Reporters.*

ples' perceptions of press credibility, or by trying to capture events that contribute to perceptions of credibility. Public opinion data about media credibility are often available through the Roper's poll. Carefully worded and sampled public surveys could capture perceived credibility as well. Measuring contributing factors to credibility is harder; not that certain kinds of things are harder to capture as data, just that their connection to perception of credibility is more tenuous. For example, erroneous stories should detract from credibility. Content analysis could be used to identify errors, error corrections, and/or debunking. Catching and prominently correcting errors should help increase credibility; the same content analysis could capture self-corrections as opposed to errors pointed out by others. However, the actual effects of such actions on credibility are often indirect or unclear.

## Measures for Attaining Public and Public Service Outcomes

Identifying outcomes and measures for the public is even more problematic than doing so for the press or the military, particularly because the "public" is an intentionally broad audience. One approach would be to assert that if the military is meeting its legal obligations and if the press has access and is meeting its 4th Estate obligations, then public goals are served. In this section, we consider three "public" outcomes: public satisfaction, the extent to which the public is an informed public, and the extent to which the public is "well-served." We discuss each below.

### Gain Information

**Satisfied with Coverage.** An attractive alternative for considering the satisfaction of the public's goals as an outcome is to assume that the public will recognize when its goals are met. If this is so, then "public satisfaction" is the relevant public outcome. This can be broken down into satisfaction with the level of coverage, satisfaction with the focus and quality of news, satisfaction with the access the press is receiving, etc. These are measured in a variety of different public opinion polls as mentioned above (as several of the press outcomes).

**Informed by Coverage.** Schudson makes a distinction between "the informed public" and the "informational public," where the former is a cornerstone of democracy and the latter is a bombardment with excesses of irrelevant information.[12] Although it is difficult to discriminate between the two, the extent to which the public is informed is an outcome worth our consideration.

There are several possible approaches to measurement. One relies on poll questions asking about the extent to which those polled are "following" a certain issue. Various polling agencies—such as the Princeton Survey Research Associates, The Pew Research Center for the People & the Press, the Harris poll, and Gallup—all ask similar questions along the lines of:

> Now I will read a list of some stories covered by news organizations this past month. As I read each item, tell me if you happened to follow this news story very **closely**, fairly **closely**, not too **closely**, or not at all **closely**. . . . The controversy over not finding weapons of mass destruction in **Iraq** so far . . . .[13]

Public opinion data are stored in such centralized data hubs as the Roper's poll at the University of Connecticut, which can be accessed through Lexis-Nexis. Another approach would be a survey asking respondents how closely they were following a certain issue or event (the war or conflict) and then ask them some specific information-content questions to confirm their knowledge. This latter approach is problematic in that it is likely to produce event-specific results; standardizing the "specific knowledge" questions across events would be a real challenge. Still, measuring the attention the public is paying to an issue is a proxy step toward measuring the extent to which the public is informed about an issue.

---

[12] Schudson, *The Power of News*.

[13] "News Interest Index" poll conducted February 11–16, 2004, n = 1,500, Roper Center at University of Connecticut, *Public Opinion Online*, accessed through Lexis-Nexis (as of July 27, 2004).

**Be "Well-Served"**

What does the public need in order to be "well-served"? This is a question that might be possible to answer in political philosophy, but as social scientists we refuse to make the heavy assumptions necessary to answer it. Even the first outcome in this section, public satisfaction, contains a strong assumption about public needs; namely, that the public recognizes them when they are met. While public satisfaction is certainly *an* outcome, it isn't necessarily equitable with the public being well-served. One can certainly imagine a public that is happy but not well-served (e.g., the famed "bread and circuses" of Rome—to keep the people of Rome from becoming too unhappy with their lives, the government provided them with enough food (bread) so they wouldn't starve and enough entertainment (circuses) so they would be amused).

While we do not have an answer to the riddle of the well-served public, we still include the outcome as a challenge and a warning. We are of the opinion that certain aspects of wartime news coverage and the way they are presented do *not* serve the public well and in fact only serve the interests of the military or, more often, the press. By trying to articulate these concerns, we hope to provoke others into thinking about good ways to consider and measure public outcomes.

A few quotes from the work of others will help us illustrate some of our concerns. The first has to do with press accountability:

> The fact that the First Amendment arguably requires no accountability by the media to the people underscores the potential for unhealthy control and domination.[14]

Though embracing and claiming a role as the 4th Estate in service to the public, the press is, in practice, not accountable to the

---

[14] Neff, Steve S., "The United States Military vs. the Media: Constitutional Friction," *Mercer Law Review,* Vol. 46, No. 2, Winter 1995. Online at http://review.law.mercer.edu/old/fr46215.htm (as of June 3, 2003).

public. This creates the potential for a classic "principal-agent" problem.[15]

The second quote concerns the lack of public value added by instantaneous and continuous war coverage:

> The "spin" the media puts on the news influences public opinion almost immediately. While the public has a right to know, does it need to know instantaneously? The author can find no public benefit to real-time news coverage of military operations other than its entertainment value. Instantaneous intelligence information only benefits military decision-makers and the enemy.[16]

The generally proposed relationship is that the press serves the public by keeping them sufficiently informed to be effective participants in democracy and by witnessing the exercise of power so that abuses will not go unnoticed. Nothing in that logic suggests that the democratic process inherently includes such a short time frame that the public must be fully informed immediately. Adamson argues, and we agree, that the public has a right to know and has a right to know in a timely fashion, but the public service roles claimed by the press are not being served by real-time coverage of events. Instead, real-time coverage provides only entertainment or intelligence to adversaries, neither of which is in the public interest.

---

[15] See Moe, Terry M., "The New Economics of Organization," *American Journal of Political Science,* Vol. 28, No. 4, November 1984, pp. 739–777, for example.

[16] Adamson, *The Effects of Real-Time News Coverage on Military Decision-Making*, p. 2.

# Bibliography

Abbott, Andrew, "Conceptions of Time and Events in Social Science Methods: Causal and Narrative Approaches," *Historical Methods*, Vol. 23, No. 4, 1990, pp. 140–150.

Adamson, William G., *The Effects of Real-Time News Coverage on Military Decision-Making,* Maxwell Air Force Base, Ala.: Air Command and Staff College, 1997.

Almond, Gabriel A., *The American People and Foreign Policy,* New York: Harcourt Brace, 1956.

Altschull, J. Herbert, *Agents of Power: The Media and Public Policy*, White Plains, N.Y.: Longman Publishers USA, 1995.

Aminzade, Ronald, "Historical Sociology and Time," *Sociological Methods & Research,* Vol. 20, No. 4, 1992, pp. 456–480.

Andrews, Peter, "The Media and the Military," *American Heritage,* Vol. 42, No. 4, July 1991, pp. 78–85.

Aukofer, Frank, and William P. Lawrence, *America's Team; the Odd Couple: A Report on the Relationship Between the Media and the Military*, Nashville, Tenn.: Freedom Forum First Amendment Center at Vanderbilt University, 1995.

Bagdikian, Ben H., "Foreword," in John R. MacArthur and Ben H. Bagdikian, *Second Front: Censorship and Propaganda in the Gulf War,* Berkeley: University of California Press, 1993.

Bagdikian, Ben H., *The Media Monopoly (4th edition)*, Boston: Beacon Press, 1992.

Baroody, Judith Raine, *Media Access and the Military: The Case of the Gulf War,* Lanham, Md.: University Press of America, 1998.

Belknap, Margaret H., "The CNN Effect: Strategic Enabler or Operational Risk?" *Parameters,* Vol. 32, No. 3, Autumn 2002, pp. 100–114.

Bennett, W. Lance, *News: The Politics of Illusion (2nd edition),* White Plains, NY: Longman, 1988.

Bennett, W. Lance, "Toward a Theory of Press-State Relations in the United States," *Journal of Communication*, Vol. 40, No. 2, Spring 1990, pp. 103–125.

Breed, Warren, "Social Control in the Newsroom: A Functional Analysis," *Social Forces,* Vol. 33, 1955, pp. 326–335.

Brightman, Carol, "In Bed with the Pentagon," *The Nation*, March 17, 2003.

Brookings Institution, *Assessing Media Coverage of the War in Iraq: Press Reports, Pentagon Rules, and Lessons for the Future,* A Brookings Iraq Series Briefing, Falk Auditorium, Washington, D.C., June 17, 2003.

Brookings Institution/Harvard Forum, *Press Coverage and the War on Terrorism Assessing the Media and the Government—A Quarterly Review,* Washington, D.C.: The Brookings Institution, January 1, 2002. Online at http://www.brookings.org/dybdocroot/comm/transcripts/20020109.htm (as of September 23, 2003).

Brownstein, Ronald, "Iraq Forcing Longer, Conventional War," *Los Angeles Times,* March 26, 2003.

Chomsky, Daniel, *One Degree Left of Center: The Mechanisms of Management Control,* Dissertation, Northwestern University, 1996.

Chomsky, Noam, and Edward Herman, *Manufacturing Consent: The Political Economy of the Mass Media,* New York: Pantheon, 1988.

Christenson, Sig, "Military to Attach Journalists to Front-Line Units If War Breaks Out," *San Antonio Express-News,* January 15, 2003.

Clarke, Victoria (presenter), *ASD PA Clarke Meeting with Bureau Chiefs,* News Transcript, Washington, D.C.: U.S. Department of Defense. October 30, 2002. Online at http://www.dod.mil/news/Nov2002/t11012002_t1030sd.html (as of September 23, 2003).

Clarke, Victoria (presenter), *Seminar on Coverage of the War on Terrorism,* News Transcript, Washington, D.C.: U.S. Department of Defense and The Brookings Institution, November 8, 2001. Online at http://www.defenselink.mil/news/Nov2001/t11182001_t1108br.html (as of September 17, 2003).

Combelles-Siegel, Pascale, *The Troubled Path to the Pentagon's Rules on Media Access to the Battlefield, Grenada to Today,* Carlisle Barracks, Pa.: U.S. Army War College Strategic Studies Institute, 1996.

Cooper, Christopher, and David Cloud, "Branches of U.S. Military Fight over Media Attention in Iraq: Armed Services Compete over Air Time and Credit; A Final Battle over Budgets?" *Wall Street Journal,* March 26, 2003.

Cooper, Kent, *The Right to Know,* New York: Farrar, Straus and Cudahy, 1956, p. 16.

Cooper, Richard T., and Paul Richter, "Former Commanders Question U.S. Strategy," *Los Angeles Times,* March 26, 2003.

Council on Foreign Relations, *Embedded Journalists in Iraq: Reality TV or Desert Mirage?* Transcript, Co-sponsored with the College of William and Mary, Washington, D.C., July 29, 2003. Online at http://www.cfr.org/publication.php?id=6189# (as of September 23, 2003).

Cross, Harold L., *The Right to Know: Legal Access to Public Records and Proceedings,* New York: Columbia University Press, 1976, pp. 2, 23–24.

Delli Carpini, Michael X., "Vietnam and the Press," in D. Michael Shafer, ed., *The Legacy: The Vietnam War in the American Imagination,* Boston: Beacon, 1990.

Dilanian, Ken, "Seeking the Inside Story in an Iraq War," *Philadelphia Inquirer,* March 16, 2003.

*DOD Dictionary of Military and Associated Terms,* Joint Publication 1-02, Washington, D.C.: Joint Chiefs of Staff, as amended through 09 June 2004.

Eisenhower, Dwight D. (1944), quoted in *Conduct of the Persian Gulf War,* Washington, D.C.: Office of the Secretary of Defense, Final Report to Congress, April 1992, p. 651. Online at http://www.ndu.edu/library/epubs/cpgw.pdf (as of September 23, 2003).

Entman, Robert, "Framing U.S. Coverage of International News: Contrasts in Narratives of the KAL and Iran Air Incidents," *Journal of Communication,* Vol. 41, No. 4, 1991, pp. 6–27.

Epstein, Edward Jay, *News from Nowhere,* Chicago: Ivan R. Dee, 1973.

Foerstel, Herbert N., *Freedom of Information and the Right to Know: The Origins and Applications of the Freedom of Information Act*, Westport, Conn.: Greenwood Press, 1999, p. 11.

Franklin, Benjamin, "Apology for Printers," in *Benjamin Franklin: Writings,* New York: Library of America, 1987, pp. 171–177.

Galloway, Joe, "Sign 'Rules for Media' or Not?" *KnightRidder,* February 20, 2003. Online at http://www.realcities.com/mld/krwashington/news/special_packages/galloway/5226190.html (as of September 23, 2003).

Gans, Herbert J., *Deciding What's News: A Study of CBS Evening News, NBC Nightly News, Newsweek and Time*, New York: Vintage Books, 1980.

Gans, Herbert J., *Democracy and the News,* Oxford, U.K.: Oxford University Press, 2003.

Gans, Herbert J., "What Can Journalists Actually Do for American Democracy?" *Press/Politics,* Vol. 3, No. 4, 1998, pp. 6–12.

Gardner, Lloyd, "America's War in Vietnam: The End of Exceptionalism?" in D. Michael Shafer, ed., *The Legacy: The Vietnam War in the American Imagination*, Boston, Mass.: Beacon, 1990.

Gartner, Michael, "Give Me Old-Time Journalism," *Quill,* Vol. 83, No. 9, November 1995.

Gauthier, Candace Cummins, "Right to Know, Press Freedom, Public Discourse," *Journal of Mass Media Ethics,* Vol. 14, No. 4, 1999, pp. 197–212.

Geneva Convention III, "Relative to the Treatment of Prisoners of War," Geneva, 1949.

Gerwehr, Scott, and Russell W. Glenn, *The Art of Darkness: Deception and Urban Operations,* Santa Monica, Calif.: RAND Corporation, MR-1132-A, 2000.

Glasgow University Media Group, *War and Peace News*, Milton Keynes, U.K.: Open University Press, 1985.

Glasser, Susan B., "Reporters Join Troops As Media and Military Try Experiment in Openness," *Washington Post*, March 7, 2003.

Goebel, Douglas J., "Military-Media Relations: The Future Media Environment and Its Influence on Military Operations," Maxwell, Ala.: Air University and Air War College, 1997.

Gowing, Nik, *Real-Time Television Coverage of Armed Conflicts and Diplomatic Crises: Does It Pressure or Distort Foreign Policy Decisions?* Cambridge, Mass.: Joan Shorenstein Barone Center on the Press Politics and Public Policy John F. Kennedy School of Government Harvard University, 1994.

Hallin, Daniel C., "The Media, the War in Vietnam, and Political Support: A Critique of the Thesis of an Oppositional Media," *The Journal of Politics,* Vol. 46, No. 1, February 1984, pp. 2–24.

Hallin, Daniel C., *The Uncensored War*, Berkeley, Calif.: University of California Press, 1986.

Haney, Patrick J., *Organizing for Foreign Policy Crises: Presidents, Advisers, and the Management of Decision Making,* Ann Arbor, Mich.: University of Michigan Press, 1997.

Hardt, Hanno, "Conflicts of Interest: New Workers, Media, and Patronage Journalism," *Media Power, Professional and Policies,* 2000, pp. 209–224.

Herman, Edward, "The Media's Role in U.S. Foreign Policy," *Journal of International Affairs,* Vol. 47, No. 1, 1993, pp. 23–45.

Hess, Stephen, "Pentagon Gamble Pays Off—So Far," reprinted from *Baltimore Sun,* April 7, 2003, by The Brookings Institution. Online at http://www.brookings.org/views/op-ed/hess/20030407.htm (as of September 23, 2003).

Hickey, Neil, "Access Denied: Pentagon's War Reporting Rules Are Toughest Ever," *Columbia Journalism Review,* Vol. 40, No. 5, Jan./Feb. 2002, pp. 26–31.

Hocking, William, *Freedom of the Press: A Framework of Principle,* Chicago, Ill.: University of Chicago, 1947, pp. 170–171.

Holohan, Anne, "Haiti 1990–6: Older and Younger Journalists in the Post–Cold War World," *Media, Culture & Society*, Vol. 25, No. 5, September 2003, pp. 691–709.

Hoon, Geoff, "No Lens Is Wide Enough to Show the Big Picture: We Are Winning, But You Wouldn't Know It from Some of the Television Reports," *London Times*, March 28, 2003.

Jentleson, Bruce W., "The Pretty Prudent Public: Post Post-Vietnam American Opinion on the Use of Military Force," *International Studies Quarterly*, Vol. 36, No. 1, March 1992, pp. 49–73.

Kampfer, John, "War Spin," *Correspondent*, BBC, first aired May 18, 2003. Online at http://news.bbc.co.uk/nol/shared/spl/hi/programmes/correspondent/transcripts/18.5.031.txt (as of September 17, 2003).

Kaniss, Phyllis, *Making Local News*, Chicago, Ill.: University of Chicago Press, 1991.

Kansteiner, Walter H., "U.S. Policy in Africa in the 1990s," in Jeremy R. Azrael and Emil A. Payin, eds., *Conference Report, U.S. and Russian Policymaking with Respect to the Use of Force*, Santa Monica, Calif.: RAND Corporation, CF-129-CRES, 1996.

King, David C., and Zachary Karabell, *The Generation of Trust: How the U.S. Military Has Regained the Public's Confidence Since Vietnam*, Washington, D.C.: The AEI Press, 2003.

Kinnard, Douglas, "Vietnam Reconsidered: An Attitudinal Survey of U.S. Army General Officers," *Public Opinion Quarterly*, Vol. 39, No. 4, Winter 1975, pp. 445–456.

Kirkland, Michael, "No 'Right' for Media to Embed with Troops," *Washington Times*, February 4, 2004.

Knickmeyer, Ellen, "Sandstorm Brings Forces to Grinding Halt," *Washington Times*, March 25, 2003.

Knightley, Phillip, *The First Casualty: From the Crimea to Vietnam: The War Correspondent As Hero, Propagandist, and Myth Maker*, Bexleyheath, U.K.: Harcourt Press, 1975.

Kurtz, Howard, "Media Notes: A Battle Plan for the '03 Campaign," *Washington Post*, January 20, 2003.

Kurtz, Howard, "Unembedded Journalist's Report Provokes Military Ire," *Washington Post*, March 27, 2003.

Larson, Eric V., *Casualties and Consensus: The Historical Role of Casualties in Domestic Support for U.S. Military Operations*, Santa Monica, Calif.: RAND Corporation, MR-726-RC, 1996.

Laurence, John, "Embedding: A Military View," *Columbia Journalism Review,* web special, May/June 2003. Online at http://www.cjr.org/year/03/2/webspecial.asp (as of September 23, 2003).

Leiby, Richard, "'Unilaterals,' Crossing the Lines: Reporters Who Venture out on Their Own Can Find the Going Deadly," *Washington Post,* March 23, 2003.

Lippman, Walter, *Essays in Public Philosophy*, Boston, Mass.: Little, Brown & Co., 1955.

Livingston, Stephen, *Clarifying the CNN Effect: An Examination of Media Effects According to Type of Military Intervention,* Cambridge, Mass.: Joan Shorenstein Center of the John F. Kennedy School of Government, Harvard University, Research Paper R-18, 1997.

Loeb, Vernon, and Thomas E. Ricks, "Questions Raised About Invasion Force: Some Ex-Gulf War Commanders Say U.S. Needs More Troops, Another Armored Division," *Washington Post*, March 25, 2003.

Lovejoy, James Kevin, "Improving Media Relations," *Military Review,* Vol. 82, No. 1, January/February 2002.

MacArthur, John R., and Ben H. Bagdikian, *Second Front: Censorship and Propaganda in the Gulf War,* Berkeley, Calif.: University of California Press, 1993.

Madison, James, *Writings of James Madison,* Vol. 9, New York: Putnam, 1910, p. 103.

Mann, Michael, *The Sources of Social Power, Vol. 1: A History of Power from the Beginning to A.D. 1760*, Cambridge, U.K.: Cambridge University Press, 1986.

Mann, Michael, *The Sources of Social Power, Vol. 2: The Rise of Classes and Nation-States, 1760–1914*, Cambridge, U.K.: Cambridge University Press, 1993.

Mattis, James N. (Commanding General, 1st Marine Division), *Operation Iraqi Freedom (OIF) Lessons Learned,* Washington, D.C.: U.S. Department of Defense, May 29, 2003, p. 33.

McCombs, Maxwell E., and Donald L. Shaw, "The Agenda Setting Function of Mass Media," *Public Opinion Quarterly,* Vol. 36, No. 2, Summer 1972, pp. 176–187.

"Media vs. Military," *Common Ground*, interview with Warren Strobel, program 9828, aired July 14, 1998. Online at http://www.commongroundradio.org/shows/98/9828.html (as of June 17, 2004).

Mermin, Jonathan, *Debating War and Peace*, Princeton, N.J.: Princeton University Press, 1999.

Mitchell, Greg, "15 Stories They've Already Bungled," 2003. Online at http://www.editorandpublisher.com/eandp/news/article_display.jsp?vnu_content_id=1850208 (as of August 5, 2003).

Moe, Terry M., "The New Economics of Organization," *American Journal of Political Science,* Vol. 28, No. 4, November 1984, pp. 739–777.

Mortensen, Frands, and Erik N. Svedsen, "Creativity and Control: The Journalist Betwixt His Readers and Editors," *Media, Culture & Society,* Vol. 2, 1980, pp. 169–177.

Moskos, Charles C., *The Media and the Military in Peace and Humanitarian Operations*, Chicago, Ill.: Robert R. McCormick Tribune Foundation, 2000.

Napoli, Philip M., "A Principal-Agent Approach to the Study of Media Organizations: Toward a Theory of the Media Firm," *Political Communication*, No. 14, Vol. 2, 1997, p. 207.

Nee, Victor, and Paul Ingram, "Embeddedness and Beyond: Institutions, Exchange, and Social Structure," in Mary C. Brinton and Victor Nee, eds., *The New Institutionalism in Sociology*, Palo Alto, Calif.: Stanford University Press, 1998.

Neff, Steve S., "The United States Military vs. the Media: Constitutional Friction," *Mercer Law Review,* Vol. 46, No. 2, Winter 1995. Online at http://review.law.mercer.edu/old/fr46215.htm (as of June 3, 2003).

O'Brien, David M., *The Public's Right to Know: The Supreme Court and the First Amendment*, New York: Praeger, 1981.

Oneal, John R., Brad Lian, and James H. Joyner, Jr., "Are the American People 'Pretty Prudent'? Public Responses to U.S. Uses of Force, 1950–1988," *International Studies Quarterly,* Vol. 40, No. 2, June 1996, pp. 261–279.

O'Neil, Robert M., "The Press and National Security: The Media and the Military: The Persian Gulf War and Beyond," *Journal of National Security Law,* Vol. 1, December 1997, pp. 1–20.

Page, Benjamin, "The Mass Media As Political Actors," *PS: Political Science and Politics,* 1996, pp. 20–24.

Parenti, Michael, *Inventing Reality: The Politics of News Media (2nd edition),* New York: St. Martin's Press, 1993.

Paul, Christopher, *Marines on the Beach: How the U.S. Arrives at Armed Intervention,* Dissertation, Los Angeles: University of California at Los Angeles, 2001.

Paul, Christopher, "The U.S. Military Intervention Decision-Making Process: Who Participates, and How?" *Journal of Political and Military Sociology,* Vol. 32, No. 1, 2004.

"Pentagon Ponders Embedded Reporter Policy," *The New York Times*, June 18, 2003.

The Pew Charitable Trusts, "No Rise in Fears or Reported Depression; Public Remains Steady in Face of Anthrax Scare," *Public Opinion and Polls,* Washington, D.C.: The Pew Research Center for the People & the Press, October 15, 2001. Online at http://www.pewtrusts.com/ideas/ideas_item.cfm?content_item_id=785&content_type_id=18 (as of June 17, 2004).

The Pew Charitable Trusts, "TV Combat Fatigue on the Rise, but 'Embeds' Viewed Favorably," *Public Opinion and Polls,* Washington, D.C.: The Pew Research Center for the People & the Press, March 28, 2003. Online at http://www.pewtrusts.com/ideas/ideas_item.cfm?content_item_id=1522&content_type_id=18 (as of June 17, 2004).

Philo, Greg, and G. McLaughlin, *The British Media and the Gulf War,* Glasgow, Scotland, U.K.: Glasgow University Media Group, 1993.

Porch, Douglas, *Media/Military Relations in the United States,* Partnership for Democratic Governance & Security, Occasional Paper # 10, July 2001. Online at http://www.pdgs.org./main-site.htm (as of September 23, 2003).

Porch, Douglas, "No Bad Stories," *Naval War College Review,* Vol. 55, No. 1, Winter 2002, pp. 85–107. Online at http://www.nwc.navy.mil/press/review/2002/winter/art5%2Dw02.htm (as of September 23, 2003).

Pounder, Gary, "Opportunity Lost: Public Affairs, Information Operations, and the Air War against Serbia," *Airpower Journal*, Vol. 14, 2000, p. 58.

Price, Vincent, and John Zaller, "Who Gets the News? Alternative Measures of News Reception and Their Implications for Research," *Public Opinion Quarterly*, Vol. 57, No. 2, Summer 1993, pp. 133–164.

Project for Excellence in Journalism, *Embedded Reporters: What Are Americans Getting?* Washington, D.C., 2003. Online at http://www.journalism.org/resources/research/reports/war/embed/default.asp (as of September 23, 2003).

*Protocol I, Additional to the Geneva Conventions of 12 August 1949, and Relating to the Protection of the Victims of International Armed Conflicts,* Geneva, 1977.

Public Relations Society of America, "Credibility Ratings for Sources of Information on Using Military Force in Foreign Affairs," *The National Credibility Index,* New York, September 1998. See http://www.prsa.org/_About/prsafoundation/nciIndex.asp?ident=prsa0 (as of February 4, 2004).

Reagan, Ronald (with Robert Lindsey), *An American Life*, New York: Simon and Schuster, 1990.

Ricchiardi, Sherry, "Preparing for War," *American Journalism Review*, March 2003.

Ricks, Thomas E., "Rumsfeld, Myers Again Criticize War Coverage; Ex-Military Officers Are Singled Out," *Washington Post*, April 18, 2003.

Ricks, Thomas E., "War Could Last Months, Officers Say," *Washington Post*, March 27, 2003.

Robinson, Piers, "The Policy-Media Interaction Model: Measuring Media Power During Humanitarian Crisis," *Journal of Peace Research,* Vol. 37, No. 5, September 2000, pp. 613–633.

Robinson, Piers, "Theorizing the Influence of Media on World Politics: Models of Media Influence on Foreign Policy," *European Journal of Communication,* Vol. 16, No. 4, 2001, pp. 523–544.

Robinson, Piers, "World Politics and Media Power: Problems of Research Design," *Media, Culture & Society,* Vol. 22, No. 2, 2000, pp. 227–232.

Rosenstiel, T., and B. Kovach, "The Journalism That Doesn't Bother to Check Its Facts," *Herald Tribune,* March 3, 1999.

Schudson, Michael, *Discovering the News: A Social History of American Newspapers*, New York: Basic Books, 1978.

Schudson, Michael, *The Power of News*, Cambridge, Mass.: Harvard University Press, 1995.

Secretary of Defense, Office of Assistant Secretary of Defense, Public Affairs, *Public Affairs Guidance (PAG) on Embedding Media During Possible Future Operations/Deployments in the U.S. Central Commands (CENTCOM) Area of Responsibility,* cable to various military and government offices, February 10, 2003.

Sewell, William H., Jr., "A Theory of Structure: Duality, Agency, and Transformation," *American Journal of Sociology,* Vol. 98, No. 1, 1992, pp. 1–29.

Shafer, Jack, "Embeds and Unilaterals," *Slate,* May 1, 2003. Online at http://slate.msn.com/id/2082412 (as of June 25, 2003).

Slavin, Barbara, and Vivienne Walt, "Allies' Pre-War Assumptions Fall Short As Iraqi Resistance Stiffens," *USA Today,* March 25, 2003.

Steger, Michael D., "Slicing the Gordian Knot: A Proposal to Reform Military Regulation of Media Coverage of Combat Operations," *University of San Francisco Law Review,* Vol. 287, Summer 1994, pp. 957–1007.

Stryker, Robin, "Beyond History Versus Theory: Strategic Narrative and Sociological Explanation," *Sociological Methods & Research*, Vol. 24, No. 3, 1996, pp. 304–352.

Thomas, Evan, "Under the Gun" *Newsweek*, Vol. 124, No. 14, October 3, 1994, p. 28.

Tischler, Barbara, "Promise and Paradox: The 1960's and American Optimism," in D. Michael Shafer, ed., *The Legacy: The Vietnam War in the American Imagination*, Boston, Mass.: Beacon, 1990.

Tuchman, Gaye, *Making News: A Study in the Construction of Social Reality*, New York: Free Press, 1978.

Tumber, Howard, "Democracy in the Information Age: The Role of the Fourth Estate in Cyberspace," *Information, Communication and Society,* Vol. 4, No. 1, 2001, pp. 95–112.

Underwood, Douglas, *When MBAs Rule the Newsroom: How the Marketers and Managers Are Reshaping Today's Media*, New York: Columbia University Press, 1993.

Venable, Barry E., "The Army and the Media," *Military Review,* January–February 2002, p. 66.

Webster, James G., and Patricia F. Phalen, *The Mass Audience: Rediscovering the Dominant Model*, Mahwah, N.J.: Erlbaum, 1997.

Wiggines, James Russell, *Freedom or Secrecy*, New York: Oxford University Press, 1956, p. 3–4.

Wolfsfeld, Gadi, *Media and Political Conflict News from the Middle East*, Cambridge, U.K.: Cambridge University Press, 1997.

Zaller, John, and Dennis Chui, "Government's Little Helper: U.S. Press Coverage of Foreign Policy Crises, 1945–1991," *Political Communication,* Vol. 13, 1996, pp. 385–405.

Zelnick, C. Robert, "The Press and National Security: Military Secrets and First Amendment Values," *Journal of National Security Law*, 1997.